Rick Steves' ®

POCKET
AMSTERDAM

W9-AKS-878

Rick Steves & Gene Openshaw

Contents

Introduction

Amsterdam of the Golden Age (the 1600s) was the world's richest city. And it's still a wonderland of canals, stately brick mansions, and carillons chiming from church spires. But the city is also a completely modern, progressive place of 820,000 people and almost as many bikes. Visitors will find no end of world-class sights: Van Gogh's *Sunflowers,* Rembrandt's self-portraits, and Anne Frank's secret hiding place.

Enjoy the city's intimate charms. Stroll quiet neighborhoods, browse bookshops, sample exotic foods, and let a local show you the right way to swallow a pickled herring. With legal marijuana and prostitution, Amsterdam exudes an earthy spirit of live and let live. Consider yourself warned...or titillated. Take it all in, then pause to watch the clouds blow past gabled rooftops—and see the Golden Age reflected in a quiet canal.

Amsterdam

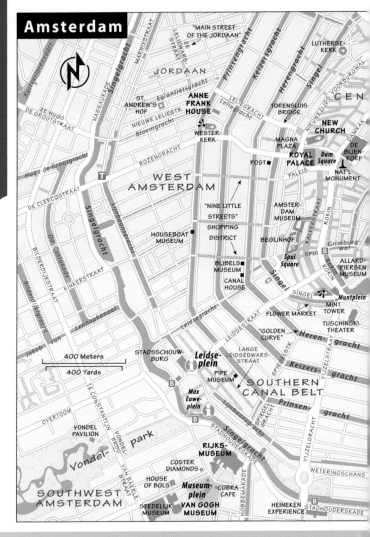

"MAIN STREET OF THE JORDAAN"

LUTHERSE-KERK

JORDAAN

Konijnenstraat

Singelgracht

Marnixstraat

2E LEIEWARS

Prinsengracht

Herengracht

Keizersgracht

Singel

CEN

Zee Hugo DE GROOTSTRAAT

Nassaukade

ST. ANDREW'S HOF

Egelantiersgracht

NIEUWE LELIESTR.

Leliegracht

Lauriergracht

TORENSLUIS BRIDGE

NIEUWEZIJDS VOORBURGWAL

NEW CHURCH

Damrak

ANNE FRANK HOUSE

Bloemgracht

WESTER-KERK

MAGNA PLAZA

ROYAL PALACE

POST

Dam Square

DE BIJENKORF

Hugo de Grootgracht

ROZENGRACHT

PALEIS.

NAT'L MONUMENT

DE CLERCQSTRAAT

WEST AMSTERDAM

T

AMSTER-DAM MUSEUM

Singelgracht

Da Costakade

Bilderdijkstraat

Kinkerstraat

"NINE LITTLE STREETS"

SHOPPING DISTRICT

Kalverstraat

Rokin

BEGIJNHOF

HOUSEBOAT MUSEUM

Bilderdijkgracht

Lennapkanaal

BIJBELS MUSEUM

CANAL HOUSE

Spui Square

SPUI

Singel

Grimburg-wal

ALLARD-PIERSEN MUSEUM

B

Leidsegracht

SINGEL

Muntplein

Rokin

Jakob van

LEIDSESTRAAT

FLOWER MARKET

MINT TOWER

MINT TOWER

TUSCHINSKI THEATER

400 Meters

400 Yards

STADSSCHOUW-BURG

Leidse-plein

"GOLDEN CURVE"

LANGE LEIDSEDWARS-STRAAT

Heren-gracht

Spiegelstr.

Vijzelstraat

PIPE MUSEUM

SOUTHERN CANAL BELT

Keizers-gracht

1E CONSTANTIJN

Max Euweplein

Prinsen-gracht

Vijzelgracht

B

Reguliersgracht

Lijnbaansgracht

Spiegelgracht

OVERTOOM

Vondelbrug

VONDEL-STRAAT

VAN BAERLE STRAAT

Stadhouderskade

Singelgracht

WETERINGSCHANS

VONDEL PAVILION

Vondel-park

RIJKS-MUSEUM

Hobbemakade

SOUTHWEST AMSTERDAM

COSTER DIAMONDS

HOUSE OF BOLS

STEDELIJK MUSEUM

Museum-plein

VAN GOGH MUSEUM

COBRA CAFE

HEINEKEN EXPERIENCE

B

Stadhouderskade

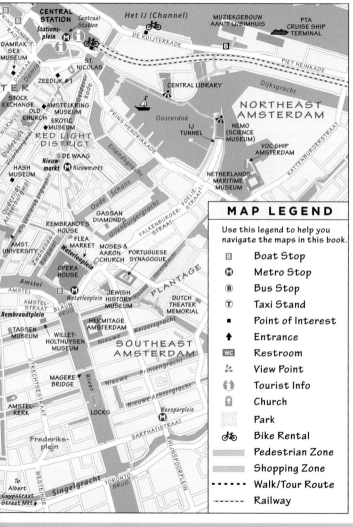

CENTRAL STATION

Het IJ (Channel)

Centraal Station

Stations-plein

PRINS HENDRIKKADE

DAMRAK SEX MUSEUM

DE RUIJTERKADE

MUZIEKGEBOUW AAN 'T IJ/BIMHUIS

PTA CRUISE SHIP TERMINAL

PIET HEINKADE

ST. NICOLAS

ZEEDIJK #1

CENTRAL LIBRARY

Dijksgracht

Geldersekade

WARMOES

STOCK EXCHANGE

OLD CHURCH

AMSTELKRING MUSEUM

EROTIC MUSEUM

RED LIGHT DISTRICT

PRINS HENDRIKKADE

Oosterdok

NORTHEAST AMSTERDAM

IJ TUNNEL

NEMO (SCIENCE MUSEUM)

VOC SHIP AMSTERDAM

KATTENBURGERSTRAAT

Oudezijds Voorburgwal

Oudezijds Achterburgwal

HASH MUSEUM

DE WAAG

Nieuw-markt

Nieuwmarkt

Eilandsgracht

NETHERLANDS MARITIME MUSEUM

Oude Schans

Kloveniersburgwal

GASSAN DIAMONDS

Uilenburgergracht

VALKENBURGER-STRAAT

FOELIE-STRAAT

AMST. UNIVERSITY

REMBRANDT'S HOUSE

FLEA MARKET

Zwanenburgwal

MOSES & AARON CHURCH

PORTUGUESE SYNAGOGUE

PLANTAGE

OPERA HOUSE

Amstel

Waterlooplein

AMSTEL-STRAAT

Rembrandtplein

BLAUW-BRUG

JEWISH HISTORY MUSEUM

Nieuwe

Keizersgracht

DUTCH THEATER MEMORIAL

TASSEN MUSEUM

WILLET-HOLTHUYSEN MUSEUM

HERMITAGE AMSTERDAM

Nieuwe

Herengracht

SOUTHEAST AMSTERDAM

UTRECHTSESTRAAT

MAGERE BRIDGE

River

Nieuwe

Prinsengracht

AMSTEL-KERK

LOCKS

Nieuwe Achtergracht

Weesperplein

Frederiks-plein

SARPHATISTRAAT

RHIJNSPOORPLEIN

To Albert Cuypstraat Street Mkt.

Singelgracht

WESTEINDE

TORONTO-BRUG

MAP LEGEND

Use this legend to help you navigate the maps in this book.

B	Boat Stop
M	Metro Stop
B	Bus Stop
T	Taxi Stand
▪	Point of Interest
♦	Entrance
WC	Restroom
½	View Point
ⓘ	Tourist Info
⛪	Church
▨	Park
🚲	Bike Rental
	Pedestrian Zone
	Shopping Zone
•••••	Walk/Tour Route
-------	Railway

About This Book

With this book, I've selected only the best of Amsterdam—admittedly, a tough call. The core of the book is six self-guided tours that zero in on Amsterdam's greatest sights and neighborhoods. The Amsterdam City Walk takes you through the heart of the city, giving you the lay of the land. At the Rijksmuseum and Van Gogh Museum, you'll see all the essentials with time left over for browsing. You'll go window-shopping in the racy Red Light District, meander the tree-lined canals of the Jordaan, and visit the Anne Frank House for insight into her tragic—but ultimately uplifting—story.

The rest of the book is a traveler's tool kit. You'll find plenty more about Amsterdam's attractions, from shopping to nightlife to less touristy sights. And there are helpful hints on saving money, avoiding crowds, getting around on Amsterdam's trams, finding a great meal, and much more.

If you'd like more information than this Pocket Guide offers, I've sprinkled the book liberally with web references. For general travel tips—as well as updates for this book—see ricksteves.com.

Amsterdam by Neighborhood

Amsterdam's Central Station (Amsterdam Centraal) sits on the north edge of the city. From here, the city spreads out like a fan in a series of concentric

Key to This Book

Sights are rated:

▲▲▲ **Don't miss**
▲▲ **Try hard to see**
▲ **Worthwhile if you can make it**
No rating **Worth knowing about**

Tourist information offices are abbreviated as **TI** and bathrooms are **WCs.**

Like Europe, this book uses the **24-hour clock.** It's the same through 12:00 noon, then keep going: 13:00 (1:00 p.m.), 14:00 (2:00 p.m.), and so on.

For opening times, if a sight is listed as "May-Oct daily 9:00-16:00," it's open from 9 a.m. until 4 p.m. from the first day of May until the last day of October.

Amsterdam's Neighborhoods

WEST AMSTERDAM

JORDAAN

ANNE FRANK HOUSE

Singelgracht

Singel

Damrak

Dam Square

CENTRAL STATION

IJ Channel

SEX

RED LIGHT DISTRICT

CENTRAL AMSTERDAM

CRUISE TERMINAL

NORTHEAST AMSTERDAM

MARITIME MUSEUM

Rokin

MINT TOWER

WATERLOO-PLEIN

JEWISH QUARTER

SOUTHERN CANAL BELT

Heren- gracht

Keizers- gracht

Prinsen- gracht

LEIDSEPLEIN

SOUTHEAST AMSTERDAM

ZOO

Amstel River

Singelgracht

Vondelpark

VAN GOGH MUSEUM

RIJKSMUSEUM

SOUTHWEST AMSTERDAM

N

500 meters

500 yards

canals. Damrak is the main north-south axis, connecting Central Station with Dam Square, the city's main square. Farther south are Leidseplein (nightlife) and the major museums (Rijksmuseum and Van Gogh).

To walk north-south through the sightseeing core—from Central Station to Dam Square to Leidseplein to the Rijksmuseum—takes about an hour.

Think of Amsterdam as a series of neighborhoods, cradling major landmarks.

Central Amsterdam: The historic core lies between Central Station and the Mint Tower/Singel canal, with Dam Square in the center. The central spine of streets (Damrak, Kalverstraat, Rokin) bustles with modern

Amsterdam at a Glance

▲▲▲**Rijksmuseum** Best collection anywhere of the Dutch Masters—Rembrandt, Hals, Vermeer, and Steen—in a spectacular setting. **Hours:** Daily 9:00-17:00. See page 35.

▲▲▲**Van Gogh Museum** 200 paintings by the angst-ridden artist. **Hours:** Daily 9:00-17:00, Fri until 22:00. See page 53.

▲▲▲**Anne Frank House** Young Anne's hideaway during the Nazi occupation. **Hours:** March 15-Sept 14 daily 9:00-21:00, Sat and July-Aug until 22:00; Sept 15-March 14 daily 9:00-19:00, Sat until 21:00; closes for Yom Kippur. See page 101.

▲▲**Stedelijk Museum** The Netherlands' top modern-art museum, recently and extensively renovated. **Hours:** Tue-Wed 11:00-17:00, Thu 11:00-22:00, Fri-Sun 10:00-18:00, closed Mon. See page 121.

▲▲**Vondelpark** City park and concert venue. **Hours:** Always open. See page 124.

▲▲**Amsterdam Museum** City's growth from fishing village to trading capital to today, including some Rembrandts and a playable carillon. **Hours:** Mon-Fri 10:00-17:00, Sat-Sun 11:00-17:00. See page 118.

▲▲**Amstelkring Museum** Catholic church hidden in the attic of a 17th-century merchant's house. **Hours:** Mon-Sat 10:00-17:00, Sun and holidays 13:00-17:00. See page 118.

▲▲**Red Light District Walk** Women of the world's oldest profession on the job. **Hours:** Best from noon into the evening; avoid late at night. See page 69.

▲▲**Netherlands Maritime Museum** Rich seafaring story of the Netherlands, told with vivid artifacts. **Hours:** Daily 9:00-17:00. See page 133.

▲▲**Hermitage Amsterdam** Russia's Tsarist treasures, on loan from St. Petersburg. **Hours:** Daily 10:00-17:00. See page 129.

▲▲**Dutch Resistance Museum** History of the Dutch struggle against the Nazis. **Hours:** Tue-Fri 10:00-17:00, Sat-Mon 11:00-17:00. See page 132.

▲**Museumplein** Square with art museums, street musicians, crafts, and nearby diamond demos. **Hours:** Always open. See page 123.

▲**Leidseplein** Lively square with cafés and street musicians. **Hours:** Always open, best on sunny afternoons. See page 126.

▲**Royal Palace** Lavish City Hall that takes you back to the Golden Age of the 17th century. **Hours:** Daily 11:00-17:00 when not closed for official ceremonies. See page 116.

▲**Begijnhof** Quiet courtyard lined with picturesque houses. **Hours:** Always open. See page 116.

▲**Hash, Marijuana, and Hemp Museum** All the dope, from history and science to memorabilia. **Hours:** Daily 10:00-23:00. See page 83.

▲**EYE Film Institute Netherlands** Film museum and cinema complex housed in a futuristic new building. **Hours:** Exhibits open daily 11:00-18:00, cinemas open roughly 10:00-24:00. See page 134.

▲**Rembrandt's House** The master's reconstructed house, displaying his etchings. **Hours:** Daily 10:00-17:00. See page 128.

▲**Diamond Tours** Offered at shops throughout the city. **Hours:** Generally daily 9:00-17:00. See page 129.

▲**Willet-Holthuysen Museum** Elegant 17th-century house. **Hours:** Mon-Fri 10:00-17:00, Sat-Sun 11:00-17:00. See page 124.

▲**Jewish Historical Museum** The Great Synagogue and exhibits on Judaism and culture, with Portuguese Synagogue across the street. **Hours:** Daily 11:00-17:00. See page 130.

▲**Dutch Theater** Moving memorial in former Jewish detention center. **Hours:** Daily 11:00-16:00. See page 131.

▲**Tropical Museum** Re-creations of tropical-life scenes. **Hours:** Tue-Sun 10:00-17:00, closed Mon. See page 132.

Houseboat Museum Your chance to see one of these floating homes from the inside. **Hours:** March-Oct Tue-Sun 11:00-17:00, closed Mon; Nov-Dec and Feb Fri-Sun 11:00-17:00, closed Mon-Thu; closed most of Jan. See page 120.

Central Library Architecturally fun spot—with great view terrace—to take a breather among Amsterdam's bookworms. **Hours:** Daily 10:00-22:00. See page 132.

chain stores and tourist sights. To the east of Damrak is the city's oldest neighborhood (De Wallen)—now the Red Light District.

West Amsterdam: West of Damrak is a pleasant area known for its four grand, tree-lined canals. Here you'll find the Anne Frank House, boutique shops, and many of my recommended hotels and restaurants. Farther west is the quieter, cozier (and mostly residential) Jordaan neighborhood.

Southern Canal Belt: The next ring of canals south of the historic core is spacious and dotted sparsely with a few intimate museums, antique shops, and recommended B&Bs. Rowdy Leidseplein anchors the lower corner.

Southwest Amsterdam: The city's major art museums (Rijksmuseum, Van Gogh, Stedelijk) and other sights cluster together on an expansive square called Museumplein. A short walk away is Vondelpark, Amsterdam's version of a Central Park. While less central, Southwest Amsterdam is easily reached by tram, so I've recommended some good-value hotels.

Southeast Amsterdam: Stretching from the edge of the Old City Center to the very outskirts, this neighborhood has a number of interesting sights, especially in the former Jewish Quarter. You'll find Rembrandt's House, a flea market, the Hermitage Amsterdam, and several Jewish-themed sights. Farther southeast (accessible by tram) are some Nazi-era sights, a zoo, and a botanical garden.

Northeast Amsterdam: East of Central Station is the newly revitalized waterfront, with the Central Library, the Netherlands Maritime Museum, and a children's science museum (NEMO).

Planning Your Time

The following day-plans give an idea of how much an organized, motivated, and caffeinated person can see. Amsterdam deserves at least three full sightseeing days.

Day 1: Follow my self-guided Amsterdam City Walk, which takes you from the train station to Leidseplein. After lunch, enjoy a relaxing canal-boat cruise. In the evening (when it's least crowded), tour the Anne Frank House.

Day 2: Visit Amsterdam's two outstanding art museums, located next to each other: the Van Gogh Museum and the Rijksmuseum. In the evening, stroll the Red Light District for some memorable window-shopping.

Daily Reminder

The biggest Amsterdam sights—
the Rijksmuseum, the Van Gogh
Museum, and the Anne Frank
House—are open daily year-
round (except the Anne Frank
House, which closes for Yom
Kippur).

Sunday: These sights have limited, afternoon-only hours
today—the Amstelkring
Museum (13:00-17:00) and Old Church (13:00-17:00). The Canal
House, Westerkerk church and tower, and the Old Church tower
are closed altogether, as is the Waterlooplein flea market.

Monday: The Stedelijk Museum, Houseboat Museum, Canal House,
the Old Church tower, and Tropical Museum are closed today.
From September through May, NEMO is closed today (but open
in peak season). Many businesses are closed Monday morning.

Tuesday: All recommended sights are open, except the Old Church
tower. The Houseboat Museum is closed off-season.

Wednesday: All recommended sights are open, except the Old Church
tower. The Houseboat Museum is closed off-season.

Thursday: All recommended sights are open. The Stedelijk Museum is
open until 22:00. The Houseboat Museum is closed off-season.

Friday: The Van Gogh Museum is open until 22:00.

Saturday: The Anne Frank House is open until 22:00 mid-March-mid-
Sept, and until 21:00 in the off-season.

Late-Night Sightseeing: The Anne Frank House stays open daily July-
Aug until 22:00. The city's naughty sights are open late every day:
the Hash, Marijuana, and Hemp Museum until 23:00, the Damrak
Sex Museum until 23:00, and the Erotic Museum until midnight
or later.

Day 3: Choose a few of these fine sights that cluster together: Amstelkring (hidden church), Rembrandt's House, Waterlooplein flea market, Gassan Diamonds (polishing demo), Willet-Holthuysen Museum, Jewish Museum, Hermitage Amsterdam, or Dutch Resistance Museum. In the afternoon, take my self-guided Jordaan Walk, and enjoy dinner in the Jordaan neighborhood.

With more time: There are plenty more small museums to visit in Amsterdam—find suggestions in the Sights chapter. Or day-trip to nearby towns such as Haarlem, Delft, or Edam.

These are busy day-plans, so be sure to schedule in slack time for picnics, laundry, people-watching, leisurely dinners, shopping, and re-charging your touristic batteries. Slow down and be open to unexpected experiences and the courtesy of the Dutch people.

Quick Tips: Here are a few tips to get you started. (You'll find more information on these topics throughout the book.) Reserve your hotel as soon as is feasible, because Amsterdam is crowded from mid-March through September. To avoid long lines, consider booking in advance for the Anne Frank House, Rijksmuseum, and Van Gogh Museum. Since opening hours are variable, get the latest information from museum web-sites, at **iamsterdam.com,** or from local publications when you arrive. A sightseeing pass, which covers admission to many sights and lets you skip ticket-buying lines, can be worthwhile for busy sightseers. Take advantage of my free Amsterdam audio tours, covering many of this book's sights. (For more details, see page 167.)

And finally, remember that although Amsterdam's sights can be crowded and stressful, the city itself is all about gentility and grace, so...be flexible.

Have a great trip!

Amsterdam City Walk

From Central Station to Leidseplein

Take a Dutch sampler walk from one end of the old center to the other, tasting all that Amsterdam has to offer along the way. It's your best single stroll through quintessentially Dutch scenes: picturesque canals, hidden churches, surprising shops, thriving happy-hour hangouts, and eight centuries of history.

The walk starts at Central Station, heads down touristy Damrak to Dam Square, and continues south down pedestrian-only Kalverstraat to the Mint Tower. Then it wafts through the flower market, before continuing south to busy Leidseplein. To return to Central Station, catch tram #2 or #5 from Leidseplein.

ORIENTATION

Length of This Walk: About 2.5 miles—allow 2.5 hours.

When to Go: Best by day, when sights are open.

Bike Rental: To make this "walk" a much faster "roll," rent a bike in Central Station (MacBike—see page 162).

Alert: Beware of silent trams (don't walk on tracks) and yield to bikes.

WCs: Try fast-food places (generally €0.30) and near the entrance to the Amsterdam Museum.

Royal Palace: €7.50, daily 11:00-17:00 but often closed for official business.

New Church: Free to view from gift-shop balcony, special exhibits-€8-15, daily 10:00-17:00.

De Papegaai Hidden Church: Free, daily 10:00-16:00.

Civic Guard Gallery: Free, daily 10:00-17:00.

Amsterdam Museum: €10, Mon-Fri 10:00-17:00, Sat-Sun 11:00-17:00.

Begijnhof: Free and always open (though churches have sporadic hours).

Audio Tour: You can download this chapter as a free Rick Steves audio tour (see page 167).

THE WALK BEGINS

❶ Central Station

Here, where today's train travelers enter the city, sailors of yore disembarked from seagoing ships. They were met by street musicians, pickpockets, hotel-runners, and ladies carrying red lanterns. Central Station, built in the late 1800s, sits on reclaimed land at what was once the harbor mouth. The station, with warm red brick and prickly spires, is the first of several Neo-Gothic buildings we'll see from the late 1800s, built during Amsterdam's economic revival. One of the towers has a clock dial; the other tower's dial is a weathervane. Watch the hand twitch as the wind gusts in every direction—N, Z, O, and W.

Let's get oriented: *noord, zuid, oost,* and *west.* Facing the station, you're facing north. Farther north, on the other side of the station, is the IJ (pronounced "eye"), the body of water that gives Amsterdam access to the open sea.

Now turn around 180 degrees and, with your back to the station, face

Central Station—gateway to the city

Damrak street—a buffet of Dutch clichés

the city, looking south. The city spreads out before you like a fan, in a series of concentric canals. Ahead of you stretches the street called Damrak, which leads to Dam Square a half-mile away. That's where we'll be heading. To the left of Damrak is the city's old *(oude)* town. More recently, that historic neighborhood has become the Red Light District (✪ see the Red Light District Walk). The big church towering above the old part of town is St. Nicholas Church. It was built in the 1880s, when Catholics—after about three centuries of oppression—were finally free to worship in public. To the right of Damrak is the new *(nieuwe)* part of town, where you'll find the Anne Frank House and the peaceful Jordaan neighborhood.

The train station is the city's transportation hub. Trams and taxis leave from out front (expect construction due to expansion of the metro). Across the street from the station is the city's main TI, marked by a *VVV* sign.

On your far right, in front of the Ibis Hotel, is a huge, multistory bikes-only **parking garage.** Biking in Holland is the way to go—the land is flat, distances are short, and there are designated bike paths everywhere. This bike parking garage is completely free, courtesy of the government, and in-tended to encourage this green and ultra-efficient mode of transportation.

▶ *Let's head out. With your back to Central Station, start walking south from the station into the city, to the top of Damrak.*

Again, be careful of trams, bikes, and cars. When you reach the head of Damrak, keep going straight, following the crowds south on Damrak, walking along the right side of the street.

❷ Damrak

This street was once a riverbed. It's where the Amstel River flowed north into the IJ, which led to a vast inlet of the North Sea called the Zuiderzee.

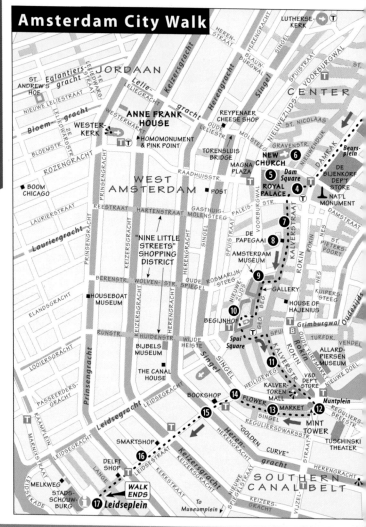

Amsterdam City Walk

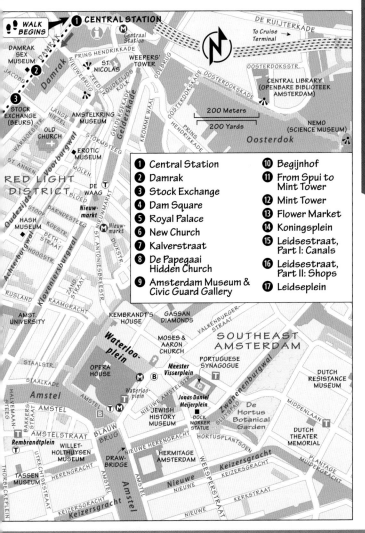

WALK BEGINS

CENTRAL STATION

DE RUIJTERKADE

To Cruise Terminal

DAMRAK SEX MUSEUM

PRINS HENDRIKKADE

WEEPERS' TOWER

ST. NICOLAS

JACOBS

Damrak

NIEUWEBRUG

ZEEDIJK

OUDEZIJDS KOLK

Centraal Station

OOSTERDOKSKADE

OSTERDOKSKADE

Oosterdoksdok

OOSTERDOKSSTR.

CENTRAL LIBRARY (OPENBARE BIBLIOTEEK AMSTERDAM)

STOCK EXCHANGE (BEURS)

LANGE NIEZEL

AMSTELKRING MUSEUM

GELDERSEKADE

KROMME WAAL

PRINS HENDRIKKADE

200 Meters

200 Yards

NEMO (SCIENCE MUSEUM)

OLD CHURCH

Voorburgwal

STORMSTEEG

Oosterdok

ST. ANNEN

EROTIC MUSEUM

MOLEN

DE WAAG

WAKMOESSTR.

RED LIGHT DISTRICT

Oudezijds

STOOF

BARNDESTEEG

BLOED

Nieuwmarkt

Nieuwmarkt

ST. ANTONIESBREESTR.

HASH MUSEUM

KOESTR.

BETH. STRAAT

HOOGSTR.

Achterburgwal

Kloveniersburgwal

ZAND-STRAAT

DIJKSTR.

RUSLAND

KLOVENIERSBURGWAL

RAAMGRACHT

AMST. UNIVERSITY

REMBRANDT'S HOUSE

GASSAN DIAMONDS

VALKENBURGER-STRAAT

MOSES & AARON CHURCH

SOUTHEAST AMSTERDAM

STAALSTR.

Waterlooplein

OPERA HOUSE

PORTUGUESE SYNAGOGUE

DUTCH RESISTANCE MUSEUM

STAALKADE

Meester Visserplein

NIEUWE AMSTELSTR.

MIDDENLAAN

HALVEMAAN-STEEG

Amstel

AMSTEL

Waterlooplein

Jonas Daniel Meijerplein

De Hortus Botanical Garden

AMSTEL

JEWISH HISTORY MUSEUM

DOCK WORKER STATUE

Zwanenburgwal

SLUYSGRACHT

BAKKERS STRAAT

AMSTELSTRAAT

BLAUW BRUG

NIEUWE HERENGRACHT

HORTUSPLANTSOEN

DUTCH THEATER MEMORIAL

Rembrandtplein

WILLET-HOLTHUYSEN MUSEUM

Herengracht

DRAW-BRIDGE

HERMITAGE AMSTERDAM

WEESPERSTRAAT

PLANTAGE MIDDENGRACHT

UTRECHTSESTRAAT

Nieuwe

Keizersgracht

KEIZERSGRACHT

TASSEN MUSEUM

HERENGRACHT

Amstel

NIEUWE

KERKSTRAAT

THORBECKEPLEIN

KEIZERSGRACHT

Keizersgracht

1 Central Station
2 Damrak
3 Stock Exchange
4 Dam Square
5 Royal Palace
6 New Church
7 Kalverstraat
8 De Papegaai Hidden Church
9 Amsterdam Museum & Civic Guard Gallery
10 Begijnhof
11 From Spui to Mint Tower
12 Mint Tower
13 Flower Market
14 Koningsplein
15 Leidsestraat, Part I: Canals
16 Leidsestraat, Part II: Shops
17 Leidseplein

It's this unique geography that turned Amsterdam into a center of trade. Boats could sail up the Amstel into the interior of Europe, or out to the North Sea, to reach the rest of the world.

Today, the Amstel is channeled into canals and its former mouth is covered by the Central Station. But Amsterdam still remains a major seaport. That's because, in the 19th century, the Dutch dug the North Sea canal. These days, more than 100,000 ships a year dock on the outskirts of Amsterdam, making it Europe's fourth-busiest seaport (including giant cruise ships). For all of Amsterdam's existence, it's been a trading center.

As you stroll along Damrak, look left. There's a marina, lined with old brick buildings. Though these aren't terribly historic buildings, the scene still captures a bit of Golden Age Amsterdam. Think of it: Back in the 1600s, this area was the harbor, and those buildings warehoused exotic goods from all over the world.

All along Damrak, you'll pass a veritable gauntlet of touristy shops. These seem to cover every Dutch cliché. You'll see wooden shoes, which the Dutch used to wear to get around easily in the marshy soil, and all manner of tulips; the real ones come from Holland's famed fresh-flower industry. Heineken fridge magnets advertise one of the world's most popular pilsner beers. You'll likely hear a hand-cranked barrel organ and see windmill-shaped saltshakers. And everything seems to be available in bright orange—the official color of the Dutch royal family.

At the **Damrak Sex Museum** (Damrak 18; ✪ see page 120), you'll find the city's most notorious commodity on display. As a port town catering to sailors and businessmen away from home, Amsterdam has always accommodated the sex trade. Continue up Damrak for more touristy delectables: Teasers (at #36) is the local Hooters. The french fry stand (#41) advertises them as *Vlaamse friets*—"Flemish fries"—as they were invented in the Low Countries. Locals dip their fries in mayonnaise, not ketchup.

Many of Damrak's eateries are ethnic. In cosmopolitan Amsterdam, international cuisine is almost like going local. Indonesia was a former Dutch colony. Here you can order *rijsttafel,* a sampler assortment of Indonesian dishes that's big enough for two. Also popular in Amsterdam are Argentinian steak houses. Amsterdammers on the go usually just grab a simple sandwich, called a *broodje* (BRODE-juh), or a pita-bread wrap, such as a *shoarma,* from a Middle Eastern take-out joint.

▸ *The long brick building with the square clock tower, along the left side of Damrak, is the...*

❸ Stock Exchange (Beurs van Berlage)

This impressive structure, a symbol of the city's long tradition as a trading town, was built with nine million bricks. Like so many buildings in this once-marshy city, it was constructed on a foundation of pilings—some 5,000 tree trunks hammered vertically into the soil. When the Beurs opened in 1903, it was one of the world's first modernist buildings, with a geometric, minimal, no-frills style. Emphasizing function over looks, it helped set the architectural tone for many 20th-century buildings.

Continuing along Damrak, make your way to the end of the long building. Though it's only a century old, Amsterdammers have gathered in this neighborhood to trade since medieval times. Back then, "trading stock" meant buying and selling goats, chickens, or kegs of beer. Over time, they began exchanging slips of paper, or "futures," rather than actual goods. Traders needed moneychangers, who needed bankers, who made money by lending money. By the 1600s, Amsterdam had become one of the world's first great capitalist cities, loaning money to free-spending kings, dukes, and bishops.

In 1984, the Beurs building was turned into a cultural center, and the stock exchange moved next door, to the Euronext complex. Amsterdam still thrives as the center of Dutch business and is home to Heineken, Shell Oil, Philips Electronics, and Unilever.

▶ *Continue along Damrak until it opens into Dam Square. Make your way—carefully—across the street to the cobblestone pavement. Now, stand in the middle of the square and take it all in.*

❹ Dam Square

Around the year 1250, some local fishermen "dammed" the "Am-stel" to make a small village called "Amstel-damme." To the north was the *damrak* (meaning "outer harbor"), a waterway that eventually led to the sea. To the south was the *rokin* (roh-KEEN, "inner harbor"), for river traffic. With access to the sea, the fishermen were soon trading with German riverboats traveling downstream and with seafaring boats from Stockholm, Hamburg, and London. Dam Square was the center of it all—the birthplace of today's Amsterdam.

Today, Dam Square is still the center of Dutch life, at least symbolically. The Royal Palace and major department stores face the square. Mimes, jugglers, and human statues mingle with locals and tourists. As Holland's

Amsterdam's Story

Visualize the physical layout of this man-made city: built on trees, protected by dikes, and laced with canals in the marshy delta at the mouth of the Amstel River. Location, location, location. Boats could arrive here from Germany by riverboat down the Rhine, from England across the Channel and down the IJ, and from Denmark by entering the Zuiderzee inlet of the North Sea. No wonder that St. Nicholas, protector of water travelers, was the city's patron saint.

As early as 1300, Amsterdam was already an international trade center of German beer, locally caught herring, cloth, bacon, salt, and wine. Having dammed and canalized the Amstel and diked out the sea tides, the Dutch drained land, sunk pilings, and built a city from scratch. When the region's leading bishop granted the town a charter (1300), Amsterdammers could then set up law courts, judge their own matters, and be essentially autonomous. The town thrived.

By 1500, Amsterdam was a walled city of 12,000, with the Singel canal serving as the moat. The city had a midcentury growth spurt when its trading rival Antwerp fell to Spanish troops, and a flood of fellow Flemish headed north, fleeing chaos and religious persecution.

In 1602, hardy Dutch sailors (and Englishman Henry Hudson) tried their hand at trade with the Far East. When they returned, they brought with them valuable spices, jewels, luxury goods...and the Golden Age.

The Dutch East India Company (abbreviated as "VOC" in Dutch), a state-subsidized import/export business, combined nautical skills with capitalist investing. With 500 or so 150-foot ships cruising in and out of Amsterdam's harbor, it was the first great multinational corporation. Amsterdam's Golden Age (c. 1600-1650) rode the wave of hard work and good fortune. Over the next two centuries, the VOC would send a half-million Dutch people on business trips to Asia, broadening their horizons.

This city of the Golden Age was perhaps the wealthiest on earth, thriving as the "warehouse of the world." Goods came from everywhere. The VOC's specialties were spices (pepper and cinnamon), coffee and tea, Chinese porcelain (delftware's Eastern inspiration), and silk. Meanwhile, the competing Dutch West India Company concentrated on the New World, trading African slaves for South American sugar. With its wealth, Amsterdam built in grand style, erecting the gabled townhouses we see today. The city expanded west and south, adding new neighborhoods.

But by 1650, Amsterdam's overseas trade was being eclipsed by new superpowers—England and France. Inconclusive wars with Louis XIV and England drained the economy, destroyed the trading fleet, and demoralized the people. Throughout the 1700s, Amsterdam was a city of backwater bankers rather than international traders, although it remained the cultural center of Holland. In early 1795, Napoleon's French troops occupied the country, and the economy was dismal.

A revival in the 1800s was spurred by technological achievements. The Dutch built a canal reconnecting Amsterdam directly with the North Sea (1824-1876), railroads laced the small country, and the city expanded southward by draining new land. The Rijksmuseum, Central Station, and Magna Plaza were built as proud monuments to the economic upswing.

The 1930s Depression hit hard, followed by five years of occupation under the Nazis, aided by pro-Nazi Dutch. The city's large Jewish population was decimated by Nazi deportations and extermination (falling from about 80,000 Jews in 1940 to just 16,000 in 1945).

With postwar prosperity, 1960s Amsterdam again became a world cultural capital as the center for Europe's hippies, who came here to smoke marijuana. Grassroots campaigns by young, artistic, politically active people promoted free sex and free bikes.

Today, Amsterdam is a city of 820,000 people jammed into small apartments (often with the same floor plan as their neighbors'). Since the 1970s, many immigrants have become locals. One in 10 Amsterdammers is Surinamese, and one in 10 prays toward Mecca.

Dam Square, with its World War II memorial, is the symbolic center of the Netherlands.

most recognizable place, Dam Square is where political demonstrations begin and end.

Circling the Square: Pan the square clockwise, and take in the sights, starting with the Royal Palace—the large domed building on the west side. To its right stands the New Church (Nieuwe Kerk). Panning past Damrak, see the proud old De Bijenkorf ("The Beehive") department store (with a nice first-floor café— ✪ see page 149).

Farther right, the Grand Hotel Krasnapolsky has a lovely circa-1900 Winter Garden. The white obelisk is the National Monument. A few blocks behind the hotel is the edge of the Red Light District. To the right of the hotel stretches the street called the Nes, lined with some of Amsterdam's edgy live-theater venues. Panning farther right, find Rokin street—Damrak's southern counterpart. Next comes the touristy Madame Tussauds, then the head of Kalverstraat, a busy pedestrian-only shopping street.

National Monument: The white obelisk was built in 1956 as a WWII memorial. The Nazis occupied Holland from 1940 to 1945; in those years they deported nearly 80,000 Jewish Amsterdammers, driving many— including young Anne Frank and her family—into hiding. Near the end of the war, the "Hunger Winter" of 1944-1945 killed thousands of Dutch and

City on a Sandbar

Amsterdam sits in the marshy delta at the mouth of the Amstel River—a completely man-made city, built on millions of wooden pilings. (The wood survives if kept wet and out of the air.) Since World War II, concrete has been used for the pilings, with foundations as deep as 120 feet.

In the Middle Ages, buildings were made of wood. But after a series of devastating fires, brick became the building material of choice. Many of the city's old buildings lean this way and that as their pilings settle.

forced many to survive on little more than tulip bulbs. The monument—with its carvings of the crucified Christ, men in chains, and howling dogs—remembers the suffering of that grim time. Now the structure is also considered a monument for peace.

❺ Royal Palace

Despite the name, this is really the former City Hall—and Amsterdam is one of the cradles of modern democracy. In medieval times, this was where the city council and mayor met. Amsterdam was a self-governing community that prided itself on its independence and thumbed its nose at royalty. In about 1650, the old medieval town hall was replaced with this one. (It rests on a foundation of 13,000 pilings.) Its style is appropriately Classical, recalling the democratic Greeks. The triangular pediment features denizens of the sea cavorting with Neptune and his gilded copper trident—all appropriate imagery for sea-trading Amsterdam.

The building became known as the "Royal Palace" in 1806, when Napoleon invaded and installed his brother Louis as king. Even after Napoleon was defeated, the victorious powers dictated that the Netherlands remain a monarchy, under a noble Dutch family called the House of Orange, who made this their home. Today, the palace is one of the four official residences of King Willem-Alexander. (Though Amsterdam is the nominal capital of the Netherlands, all governing activity—and the King's actual permanent home—are in The Hague, 30 miles away.) The Royal Palace is usually open to visitors (✪ see page 116).

Royal Palace on Dam Square

New Church, where monarchs are crowned

❻New Church (Nieuwe Kerk)

Though called the "New" Church, this building is actually 600 years old—a mere 100 years newer than the "Old" Church in the Red Light District. The sundial above the entrance once served as the city's official timepiece.

Interior: While it's pricey to enter the church, cheapskates can get a glimpse for free. Enter through the gift shop (just to the left of the main church entrance), and climb the stairs to a balcony with a small free museum and great views of the nave.

The church's bare, spacious, well-lit interior (occupied by a new art exhibit every three months) looks quite different from the Baroque-encrusted churches found in the rest of Europe. In 1566, clear-eyed Protestant extremists throughout Holland marched into Catholic churches (including this one), lopped off the heads of holy statues, stripped gold-leaf angels from the walls, urinated on Virgin Marys, and shattered stained-glass windows in a wave of anti-Catholic vandalism.

This iconoclasm (icon-breaking) of 1566 started an 80-year war against Spain and the Habsburgs, leading finally to Dutch independence in 1648. Catholic churches like this one were converted to the new dominant religion, Calvinist Protestantism (today's Dutch Reformed Church). From then on, Dutch churches downplayed the "graven images" and "idols" of ornate religious art.

Take in the church's main highlights. At the far left end is an organ from 1655, still played for midday concerts. Opposite the entrance, a stained-glass window shows Count William IV giving the city its "XXX" coat of arms. The window over the entrance portrays the inauguration of Queen Wilhelmina, who became the steadfast center of the Dutch Resistance during World War II. The choir, once used by the monks, was, after the

Reformation, turned into a mausoleum for a great Dutch admiral.

This church is where many of the Netherlands' monarchs are married, and all are "inaugurated." (Dutch royals never actually wear the official crown.) In April of 2013, Willem-Alexander—Wilhelmina's great-grandson—paraded through this church to the golden choir screen, where he was presented with the royal crown, scepter, orb, sword—and a copy of the Dutch constitution—and, with TV lights glaring and cameras flashing, was sworn in as the new sovereign.

▶ *From Dam Square, head south (at the Rabobank sign) on...*

❼ Kalverstraat

This shopping street (strictly pedestrian-only—even bikers need to dismount and walk) has been a traditional shopping street for centuries. But today it's notorious among locals as a noisy ghetto with chain stores and no soul. For smaller and more elegant stores, try the adjacent district called De Negen Straatjes ("The Nine Little Streets"). Only about four blocks west of Kalverstraat, it's where 200 or so shops and cafés mingle along pleasant canals.

▶ *About 100 yards along, keep a sharp eye out for the next sight (it's fairly easy to miss): On the right, just before and across from the McDonald's, at #58. Now pop into...*

❽ De Papegaai Hidden Church (Petrus en Paulus Kerk)

This Catholic church is an oasis of peace amid crass 21st-century commercialism. It's not exactly a hidden church (after all, you've found it), but it still keeps a low profile. That's because it dates from an era when Catholics in Amsterdam were forced to worship in secret.

In the 1500s, as Protestants were fighting Catholics all over Europe, Amsterdam was taken over by Protestant extremists. For the next two centuries, Catholic worship was illegal, though it was tolerated so long as it was practiced in humble, unadvertised places, like this church.

▶ *Continue south on Kalverstraat for about 100 yards. At #92, where Kalverstraat crosses Wijde Kapel Steeg, turn right to enter the complex housing the...*

❾ Amsterdam Museum and Civic Guard Gallery (Schuttersgalerij)

You enter the Amsterdam Museum complex under an archway with Amsterdam's coat of arms. The X-shaped crosses on the red shield represent (not the sex trade, but...) the crucifixion of St. Andrew, the patron saint of fishermen. The crown is the Habsburg royal crown, granted to Amsterdam as thanks for a loan from Dutch bankers.

Continue under the arch, past a pleasant café, a shaded courtyard, and a pay WC. Up ahead is the **Amsterdam Museum** (✪ described on page 118).

But we'll turn left, into the Civic Guard Gallery—a free, glassed-in passageway lined with paintings. (If it's closed, you'll need to backtrack to Kalverstraat and continue south, then turn right on Begijnensteeg, to find our next stop, the Begijnhof).

Civic Guard Gallery (Schuttersgalerij): This hall features group portraits from Amsterdam's Golden Age, the early 1600s. Giant statues of Goliath and a knee-high David (from 1650) watch over the whole thing.

Stroll around and gaze into the eyes of the hardworking men and women who made tiny Holland so prosperous and powerful. These are ordinary middle-class people, merchants, and traders, dressed in their Sunday best. They come across as good people—honest, businesslike, and friendly.

The Dutch got rich the old-fashioned way—they earned it. With colonies stretching from India to Indonesia, to "Nieuw Amsterdam" (today's New York), Holland's merchant fleets ruled supreme by 1600. The trading ships were financed by a new generation of clever businessmen back home in Amsterdam.

The portraits show proud men gathered with their Civic Guard militia units. These units defended Holland, but they were also fraternal organizations of business bigwigs—the Rotary Clubs of the 17th century. The weapons they carry—pikes and muskets—are mostly symbolic.

The Amsterdam Museum's entrance arch

Civic Guard group portrait—"Say *kaas.*"

Many paintings look the same in this highly stylized genre. The men usually sit arranged in two rows. Someone holds the militia's flag. Later group portraits showed "captains" of industry going about their work, dressed in suits, along with the tools of their trade—ledger books, quill pens, and money.

Everyone looks straight out, and every face is lit perfectly. Each paid for his own portrait and wanted it right. It took masters like Rembrandt and Frans Hals to take the starch out of the collars and compose more natural scenes.

Find Ervin Olaf's "Dutch School" painting. It's a fun look at the city's cultural leaders in 2006, posing as Golden Age bigwigs.

▸ *Exit out the far end of the Civic Guard Gallery. Once in the light of day, continue ahead one block farther south and find the humble gate on the right, at the...*

❿ Begijnhof

As you enter, keep in mind that this spot isn't just a tourist attraction; it's also a place where people live. Be considerate: Don't photograph the residents or their homes, and if you're here in the evening, be quiet and stick to the area near the churches.

This quiet courtyard, lined with houses around a church, has sheltered women since 1346. This was the home of a community of Beguines—pious and simple women who removed themselves from the world at large to dedicate their lives to God.

Just beyond the church you'll find a **statue** of one of these charitable sisters. Poor and rich women alike turned their backs on materialism and marriage to live here in Christian poverty, serving others. The Beguines' ranks swelled during the Golden Age, when so many women were widowed by the hazards of overseas trade. Though obedient to a mother superior, the members of the lay order of Beguines were not nuns. They spent their days deep in prayer, spinning wool, making lace, teaching, and caring for the sick.

The last Beguine died in 1971, but this Begijnhof still provides subsidized housing to about 100 single women, mostly Catholic seniors. The Begijnhof is just one of a few dozen *hofjes* (little housing projects surrounding courtyards) that dot Amsterdam.

Now turn your attention to the brick-faced **English Reformed church** (Engelse Kerk), built in 1420 to serve the Beguine community. In

Begijnhof—quiet courtyard for lay sisters   Begijn statue by the Pilgrim church

1607, the church became Anglican. The church served as a refuge for English traders and religious refugees fleeing persecution in England. Strict Protestants such as the famous Pilgrims stopped here in tolerant Amsterdam, praying in this church before sailing to religious freedom in America. If the church is open, step inside, and head to the far end, toward the stained-glass window. It shows the Pilgrims praying before boarding the Mayflower. Along the right-hand wall is an old pew they may have sat on, and on the altar is a Bible from 1763, with lots of old-style ſ's.

Back outside, find the **Catholic church,** which faces the English Reformed Church. Because Catholics were being persecuted when it was built, this had to be a low-profile, "hidden" church—notice the painted-out windows on the second and third floors. Step inside, through the (literally) low-profile doorway. It's decorated lovingly, if on the cheap (try tapping softly on a "marble" column). Amsterdam's Catholics must have eagerly awaited the day when they were legally allowed to say Mass (that day finally came in the 19th century).

Today, Holland still has something of a religious divide, but not a bitter one. Amsterdam itself is pretty un-churched. But the Dutch countryside is much more religious, including a "Bible Belt" region where 98 percent of the population is Protestant. Overall, in the Netherlands, the country is divided fairly evenly between Catholics, Protestants, and those who see Sunday as a day to sleep in and enjoy a lazy brunch.

Back outside, find the black **wooden house** (at #34), the city's oldest, from 1477. Originally, the whole city consisted of wooden houses like this one. They were eventually replaced with brick houses, to minimize the fire danger.

▸ *Near the wooden house, find a little corridor leading you back into the modern world. Head up a few steps to emerge into a lively square called Spui. Turn left, and walk two blocks to busy Kalverstraat.*

⑪ From Spui to the Mint Tower

Spui (spow, rhymes with cow), lined with cafés and bars, is one of the city's more popular spots for nightlife and sunny afternoon people-watching.

(*Optional Detour:* A block farther east of Kalverstraat is the street called Rokin, the Rondvaart Kooij canal cruise, and—for cigar connoisseurs—the House of Hajenius cigar store, at Rokin 92.)

Head south on Kalverstraat. The **Vroom & Dreesmann** department store is where ordinary locals go for basic supplies. Its cheap cafeteria (La Place, ✪ see page 149) is handy for a lunch break. The **Kalvertoren** complex is a modern mall. Inside, the slanting glass elevator takes people to the top floor, to enjoy something that's rare in altitude-challenged Amsterdam—a nice view.

▶ *Kalverstraat leads directly to Muntplein, with...*

⑫ The Mint Tower (Munttoren)

The tower with the clock once marked the limit of the old walled city, and served as one of its original gates. In the Middle Ages, the city walls were here, girdled by a moat—the Singel canal. Until about 1500, the area beyond here was nothing but marshy fields and a few farms on reclaimed land. The Mint Tower's steeple was added later—in the year 1620, as you can see written below the clock face.

Today, the tower is a favorite within Amsterdam's marijuana culture. Stoners love to take a photo of the clock and its 1620 sign at exactly 4:20 p.m. Why? Because 4:20 is the universally recognized time when work ends, and you fire up a joint. And on the 24-hour clock, 4:20 p.m. is 16:20... Du-u-u-ude!

▶ *Continue past the Mint Tower, first walking a few yards south along busy Vijzelstraat (keep an eye out for trams). Then turn right and walk west along the south bank of the Singel canal. The canal is lined with the greenhouse shops of the...*

⑬ Flower Market (Bloemenmarkt)

The stands along this busy block sell cut flowers, plants, bulbs, seeds, and garden supplies. Browse your way toward the end of the block.

The Bloemenmarkt is a testament to Holland's long-time love

The Mint Tower once marked the border of the medieval, walled city.

"Tulip mania" lives on at the Flower Market.   Be daring—try a herring.

affair with flowers. The Netherlands is by far the largest flower exporter in Europe, and a major force worldwide. If you're looking for a souvenir, note that certain seeds are marked as OK to bring back through customs into the US (the marijuana starter-kit-in-a-can is probably...not).

The best-known Dutch flower, the tulip, was brought from central Asia in the late-1500s. The hardy bulbs thrived in the sandy soil of Holland's re-claimed land. Within a generation, tulips grew from a nice luxury into an all-out frenzy. Soon, a single prized bulb could sell for the equivalent of thousands of dollars. By 1637, it was full-blown "Tulip mania"—yes, that's what even the Dutch called it. Then the tulip bubble burst. Overnight, once-wealthy investors were broke. The crash was devastating, even playing a role in the decline of the Golden Age. But Holland's love of this delightful flower lived on. Today, tulips are a major industry, and are firmly planted in the Dutch psyche.

▶ *The long Flower Market ends at the next bridge, where you'll see a square named* ⓮ **Koningsplein.** *Here there's a popular herring stand. The sign* Hollandse nieuwe *means the herring are "new" (fresh), caught during the May-June season. Amsterdammers like to eat the fish whole—you grab it by the tail, tip your head back, and down she goes.*

From Koningsplein, turn left, heading straight south (past the Selexyz bookstore) until Koningsplein leads into the street called Leidsestraat.

⓯ Leidsestraat, Part I: Canals

The first of several grand canals you'll pass is Herengracht.

Looking left down Herengracht, you'll see the so-called **"Golden Curve"** of the canal. It's lined with townhouses sporting especially nice gables. Amsterdam has many different types of gables—bell-shaped,

Leidsestraat—busy with trams and shoppers

Delftware—blue-painted ceramics

step-shaped, and so on. This stretch is best known for its "cornice" gables (straight across). These topped the Classical-looking facades of rich merchants—the *heren*. (For more on gables, see the sidebar on page 91.)

There are so many canals in Amsterdam because the city was founded in a marshy river delta, so they needed to keep the water at bay. They dammed the Amstel River and channeled it safely away into canals, creating pockets of dry land to build on.

The word *gracht* (pronounced, roughly, "khrockt," but with guttural flair) means canal. Today, the city has about 100 canals. Most are about 10 feet deep. They're crossed by some 1,200 bridges, fringed with 100,000 Dutch-elm and lime trees, and lined by 2,500 houseboats. A system of locks (back near the Central Station) controls the flow. The locks are opened periodically to flush out the system.

Leidsestraat is a busy street, crowded with shoppers, tourists, bicycles, and trams (keep your wits about you along here, and don't walk on the tram tracks). Notice that, as the street narrows, trams must wait their turn to share a single track.

▶ *Cross over the next canal (Keizersgracht), then find the little shop called "When Nature Calls," on the right at Kaisersgracht 508.*

⑯ Leidsestraat, Part II: Shops

"When Nature Calls" is a so-called "smartshop." Smartshops are fully licensed businesses that sell drugs—some of them quite strong, most of them illegal back home, and not all of them harmless. But since all these products are found in nature, the Dutch government considers them legal. (For more on smartshops, ✪ see page 71). You can check out the window displays, or go on in and browse.

Continue along Leidsestraat. Where Leidsestraat crosses Prinsengracht, just over the bridge on the right, you'll find **The Delft Shop** (at Prinsengracht 440). This place sells good examples of the glazed ceramics known as delftware, famous for its distinctive blue-and-white design. It's traditionally made in Delft, a quaint town about 30 miles southwest of here. Dutch traders learned the technique from the Chinese of the Ming dynasty, and many pieces have an Oriental look. The doodads with arms branching off a trunk are popular "flower pagodas," vases for displaying tulips.

▶ *Continue down Leidsestraat past more shops—both high-fashion and tacky tourist places—until you reach the big, busy square, called...*

⑰ Leidseplein

This is Amsterdam's liveliest square: filled with outdoor tables under trees; ringed with cafés, theaters, and nightclubs; bustling with tourists, diners, trams, mimes, and fire-eaters. No wonder locals and tourists alike come here day and night, to sit under the trees, sip a coffee or beer, in the warmth of the sun or the glow of lantern light.

Do a 360-degree spin: Leidseplein's south side is bordered by the huge Apple Store—sitting on what may be the city's most expensive piece of real estate. Nearby is the city's main serious theater, the Stadsschouwburg. Tucked inside the theater is the AUB/Last Minute Ticket Shop, a handy box office. It sells tickets for all kinds of shows around town, including half-price, same-day tickets to select shows (after 12:00 Fri-Sat only).

To the right of the Stadsschouwburg is a lane leading to the **Melkweg** ("Milky Way") nightclub. Back in the 1970s, this place was almost mythical—an entertainment complex entirely devoted to the young generation and their desires.

Continue panning to the right. The neighborhood beyond Burger King is Amsterdam's **"Restaurant Row,"** featuring Thai, Brazilian, Indian, Italian, Indonesian—and even a few Dutch—eateries.

Next, on the east end of Leidseplein, is the **Bulldog Café and Coffeeshop,** the flagship of several coffeeshops in town with the Bulldog name. (Notice the sign above the door: It once housed the police bureau.) A small green-and-white decal on the window indicates that it's a city-licensed "coffeeshop," where marijuana is sold and smoked legally. Incredible as that may seem to visitors from the States, it's been going

The Bulldog Café coffeeshop on Leidseplein, a place to kick back after this walk.

on here in Amsterdam for over 30 years—another Dutch cliché alongside windmill peppermills and wooden shoes.

▶ *Our walk is over. But those with more energy could get out their maps and make their way to Vondelpark or the Rijksmuseum. To return to Central Station (or to nearly anyplace along this walk), catch tram #2 or #5 from Leidseplein.*

Rijksmuseum Tour

At Amsterdam's Rijksmuseum ("Rijks" rhymes with "bikes"), Holland's Golden Age shines with the best collection anywhere of the Dutch Masters—from Vermeer's quiet domestic scenes, to Steen's raucous family meals, to Hals' snapshot portraits, to Rembrandt's moody brilliance.

The 17th century saw the Netherlands at the pinnacle of its power. Trade and shipping boomed, wealth poured in, and the arts flourished. Upper-middle-class businessmen hired artists to paint their portraits and decorate their homes with pretty still lifes and nonpreachy, slice-of-life art.

Dutch art is meant to be enjoyed, not studied. It's straightforward, meat-and-potatoes art for the common man. On this visit, we'll enjoy the beauty of everyday things rendered in exquisite detail. Set your cerebral cortex on "low" and let the art pass straight from the eyes to the heart, with minimal detours.

ORIENTATION

Cost: €15, not covered by I amsterdam Card.

Hours: Daily 9:00-17:00, last entry 30 minutes before closing.

Advance Tickets: You can avoid 30-minute ticket-buying lines by buying in advance online at www.rijksmuseum.nl, or from many hotels. Tickets bought in advance are good any time (no entry time specified). Buying online also lets you scoot to the front of the security line.

Avoiding Crowds: The museum is most crowded from April to September (especially April-June), on weekends, and during morning hours. It's least crowded after 15:00.

Getting There: From Central Station, catch tram #2 or #5 (get off at Hobbemastraat). The museum entrance is located inside the public passageway that runs right through the center of the building.

Services: In the reception area called the Atrium, you'll find a helpful info desk (with free maps), free baggage check, videoguide rental, WCs, cafés, and a gift shop.

Information: Tel. 020/674-7047, rijksmuseum.nl.

Length of This Tour: Allow 1.5 hours.

Cuisine Art: The Rijksmuseum Grand Café is in the Atrium. (No museum ticket required to eat here.) Beyond the museum complex, you'll find the Cobra Café on Museumplein (daily 10:00-18:00, tel. 020/470-0111). Vondelpark and Museumplein are perfect for picnics.

Photography: Permitted but no flash.

Starring: Rembrandt van Rijn, Frans Hals, Johannes Vermeer, Jan Steen.

The Rijksmuseum, on pleasant Museumplein

The Atrium has tourist services.

THE TOUR BEGINS

▶ *From the lower level Atrium, pass through security and follow the crowds up the stairway on your left. Keep climbing to the second floor, arriving at the Great Hall. With its stained-glass windows and vaulted ceiling, this place feels like a cathedral of Dutch art. Now, follow the flow into the...*

Gallery of Honor

This grand space was purpose-built to hold the Greatest Hits of the Golden Age, by the era's biggest rock stars: Frans Hals, Vermeer, Jan Steen, and Rembrandt. The best of the era's portraits, still lifes, landscapes, and slice-of-life "genre scenes" give us a close-up look at everyday life in this happy, affluent era.

Frans Hals (c. 1581-1666)

Frans Hals was the premier Golden Age portrait painter. Merchants hired him the way we'd hire a wedding photographer. With a few quick strokes, Hals captured not only the features, but also the personality.

The Merry Drinker (1627)

You're greeted by a jovial man in a black hat (✪ see photo on page 35), capturing the earthy, exuberant spirit of the Dutch Golden Age. Notice the details—the happy red face of the man offering us a glass of wine, the sparkle in his eyes, the lacy collar, the decorative belt buckle, and so on.

Now move in closer. All these meticulous details are accomplished with a few thick, messy brushstrokes. The beard is a tangle of brown worms, the belt buckle a yellow blur. His hand is a study in smudges. Even the expressive face is created with a few well-chosen patches of color. Unlike the still-life scenes, this canvas is meant to be viewed from a distance, where the colors and brushstrokes blend together.

Rather than posing his subject, making him stand for hours saying "cheese," Hals tried to catch him at a candid moment. He often painted common people, fishermen, and barflies, such as this one. He had to work quickly to capture the serendipity of the moment. Hals used a stop-action technique, freezing the man in mid-gesture, where the rough brushwork creates a blur that suggests the man is still moving.

Two centuries later, the Impressionists learned from Hals' messy brushwork. In the Van Gogh Museum, you'll see how Van Gogh painted,

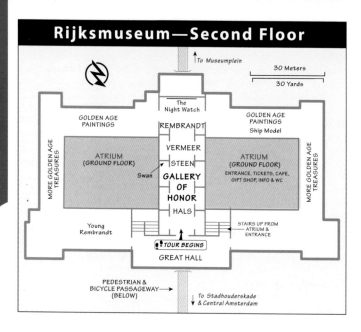

Rijksmuseum—Second Floor

↑ To Museumplein

30 Meters
30 Yards

GOLDEN AGE PAINTINGS

GOLDEN AGE PAINTINGS

Ship Model

The Night Watch

REMBRANDT

VERMEER

STEEN

← Swan

GALLERY

OF

HONOR

HALS

ATRIUM (GROUND FLOOR)

ATRIUM (GROUND FLOOR)

ENTRANCE, TICKETS, CAFE, GIFT SHOP, INFO & WC

MORE GOLDEN AGE TREASURES

MORE GOLDEN AGE TREASURES

Young Rembrandt

STAIRS UP FROM ATRIUM & ENTRANCE →

TOUR BEGINS

GREAT HALL

PEDESTRIAN & BICYCLE PASSAGEWAY → (BELOW)

↓ To Stadhouderskade & Central Amsterdam

say, a brown beard by using thick dabs of green, yellow, and red that blend at a distance to make brown.

Wedding Portrait of Isaac Abrahamsz Massa and Beatrix van der Laen (1622)

This wedding portrait of a chubby, pleasant merchant and his bride sums up the story of the Dutch Golden Age. Because this overseas trader was away from home for years at a time on business, Hals makes a special effort to point out his patron's commitment to marriage. Isaac pledges allegiance to his wife, putting his hand on his heart. Beatrix's wedding ring is prominently displayed dead center between them (on her right-hand forefinger, Protestant-style). The vine clinging to a tree is a symbol of man's support and woman's dependence. And in the distance at right, in the classical love garden, are other happy couples strolling arm-in-arm amid peacocks, a symbol of fertility.

In earlier times, marriage portraits put the man and wife in separate

The Dutch Golden Age (1600s)

Who bought this art? Look around at the Rijksmuseum's many portraits, and you'll see ordinary middle-class people, merchants, and traders. Even in their Sunday best, you can tell that these are hardworking, businesslike, friendly, simple people (with a penchant for wearing ruffed collars).

By 1600, Holland's merchant fleets ruled the waves with colonies as far away as India, Indonesia, and America (remember—New York was originally "Nieuw Amsterdam"). Back home, these traders were financed by shrewd Amsterdam businessmen on the new frontiers of capitalism. With their newfound wealth, the Dutch bought art.

Look around again. Is there even one crucifixion? One saint? One Madonna? In most countries, Catholic bishops and rich kings supported the arts. But the Republic of the Netherlands was independent, democratic, and largely Protestant, with no taste for saints and Madonnas.

Instead, Dutch burghers bought pretty, unpreachy, unpretentious works for their homes—portraits of themselves, still lifes (of food and mundane objects), landscapes, and "genre" scenes from everyday life.

canvases, staring out grimly. Hals' jolly side-by-side couple reflects a societal shift from marriage as business partnership to an arrangement that's more friendly and intimate.

Hals didn't need symbolism to tell us that these two are prepared for their long-distance relationship—they seem relaxed together, but each looks at us directly, with a strong, individual identity. Good as gold, these are the type of people who propelled this soggy little country into its glorious Golden Age.

Johannes Vermeer (1632-1675)

Vermeer is the master of tranquility and stillness. He creates a clear and silent pool that is a world in itself. Most of his canvases show interiors of Dutch homes, where Dutch women engage in everyday activities, lit by a side window.

Vermeer's father, an art dealer, gave Johannes a passion for painting. Late in the artist's career, with Holland fighting draining wars against England, the demand for art and luxuries went sour in the Netherlands, forcing Vermeer to downsize—he sold his big home, packed up his wife and 14 children, and moved in with his mother-in-law. He died two years later, and his works fell into centuries of obscurity.

The Rijksmuseum has the best collection of Vermeers in the world—four of them. (There are only some 34 in captivity.) Each is a small jewel worth lingering over.

The Milkmaid (c. 1658)

It's so quiet you can practically hear the milk pouring into the bowl.

Vermeer brings out the beauty in everyday things. The subject is ordinary—a kitchen maid—but you could look for hours at the painting's tiny details and rich color tones. These are everyday objects, but they glow in a diffused light: the crunchy crust, the hanging basket, even the rusty nail in the wall with its tiny shadow. Vermeer had a unique ability with surface texture, to show how things feel when you touch them.

The maid is alive with Vermeer's distinctive yellow and blue—the colors of many traditional Dutch homes—against a white backdrop. She is content, solid, and sturdy, performing this simple task as if it's the most important thing in the world. Her full arms are built with patches of reflected

Vermeer's *Milkmaid*—quiet beauty

Woman Reading a Letter—from whom?

Shhh...Dutch Art

You're sitting at home late one night, and it's perfectly calm. Not a sound, very peaceful. And then...the refrigerator motor turns off, and it's really quiet.

Dutch art is really quiet art. It silences our busy world, so that every sound, every motion is noticeable. You can hear cows tearing off grass 50 yards away. You notice how the cold night air makes the stars sharp.

In fact, one of the museum's most dramatic, over-the-top paintings is probably *The Threatened Swan* (in the Gallery of Honor). It's quite a contrast to the rape scenes and visions of heaven of Italian Baroque paintings from the same time period.

light. Vermeer squares off a little world in itself (framed by the table in the foreground, the wall in back, the window to the left, and the footstool at right), then fills this space with objects for our perusal.

Woman Reading a Letter (c. 1662-1663)

This painting likely will be away for renovation during your visit. If you do get to see it on display, notice how Vermeer's placid scenes often have an air of mystery. The woman is reading a letter. From whom? A lover? A father on a two-year business trip to Indonesia? Not even taking time to sit down, she reads it intently, with parted lips and a bowed head. It must be important. (She looks pregnant, adding to the mystery, but that may just be the cut of her clothes.)

Again, Vermeer has framed a moment of everyday life. But within this small world are hints of a wider, wilder world—the light coming from the left is obviously from a large window, giving us a whiff of the life going on outside. The map hangs prominently, reminding us of travel, and perhaps of where the letter is from.

The Love Letter (c. 1669-1670)

There's a similar theme here. The curtain parts, and we see through the doorway into a dollhouse world, then through the seascape on the back wall to the wide ocean. A woman is playing a lute when she's interrupted by

Vermeer's *The Love Letter* | Scene from the artist's hometown of Delft

a servant bringing a letter. The mysterious letter stops the music, intruding like a pebble dropped into the pool of Vermeer's quiet world. The floor tiles create a strong 3-D perspective that sucks us straight into the center of the painting—the woman's heart.

View of Houses in Delft (a.k.a. *The Little Street*, c. 1658)

Vermeer was born in the picturesque town of Delft, grew up near its Market Square, and set a number of his paintings there. This may be the view from his front door.

In *The Little Street,* the details actually aren't very detailed—the cobblestone street doesn't have a single individual stone in it. But Vermeer shows us the beautiful interplay of colored rectangles on the buildings. Our eye moves back and forth from shutter to gable to window...and then from front to back, as we notice the woman deep in the alleyway.

Jan Steen (1626-1679)

Not everyone could afford a masterpiece, but even poorer people wanted works of art for their own homes (like a landscape from Sears for over the sofa). Jan Steen (pronounced "yahn stain"), the Norman Rockwell of his day, painted humorous scenes from the lives of the lower classes. As a tavern owner, he observed society firsthand.

The Burgher of Delft and His Daughter (1655)

This painting is the latest major acquisition of the Rijksmuseum and another star in its lineup. In August of 2004, the museum paid $15 million for it...and figured they got a great deal. While the rest of the Steen collection is in the next room, the curators often display this one with Vermeer's works

Ruffs

I cannot tell you why men and women of the Dutch Golden Age found these fanlike collars attractive, but they certainly were all the rage here and elsewhere in Europe. It started in Spain in the 1540s, but the style really took off with a marvelous discovery in 1565: starch. Within decades, Europe's wealthy merchant class was wearing nine-inch collars made from 18 yards of material.

The ruffs were detachable and made from a long, pleated strip of linen set into a neck (or wrist) band. You tied it in front with strings. Big ones required that you wear a wire frame underneath for support. There were various types—the "cartwheel" was the biggest, a "double ruff" had two layers of pleats, and a "cabbage" was somewhat asymmetrical.

Ruffs required elaborate maintenance. First, you washed and starched the linen. While the cloth was still wet, hot metal pokers were painstakingly inserted into the folds to form the characteristic figure-eight pattern. The ruffs were stored in special round boxes to hold their shape.

For about a century, Europeans loved the ruff, but by 1630, Holland had come to its senses, and the fad faded.

because it's pristine and peaceful—more like an exquisite Vermeer than a raucous Steen.

Steen's well-dressed burgher sits on his front porch, when a poor woman and child approach to beg, putting him squarely between the horns of a moral dilemma. On the one hand, we see his rich home, well-dressed daughter, and a vase of flowers—a symbol that his money came from morally suspect capitalism (the kind that produced the folly of 1637's "tulip mania", ✪ described on page 31). On the other hand, there are his poor fellow citizens and the church steeple, reminding him of his Christian

Steen—a rich burgher's moral dilemma

Steen—playful family scene at Christmas

duty. The man's daughter avoids the confrontation. Will the burgher set the right Christian example? This moral dilemma perplexed many nouveau-riche Dutch Calvinists of Steen's day.

This early painting by Steen demonstrates his mastery of several popular genres: portrait, still life (the flowers and fabrics), cityscape, and moral instruction.

The Feast of St. Nicholas

It's Christmas time, and the kids have been given their gifts, including a little girl who got a doll. The mother says, "Let me see it," but the girl turns away playfully. Everyone is happy except the boy, who's crying. His Christmas present is only a branch in his shoe—like coal in your stocking, the gift for bad boys. His sister gloats and passes it around. The kids laugh at him. But wait—it turns out the family is just playing a trick. In the background, the grandmother beckons to him, saying, "Look, I have your real present in here." Out of the limelight, but smack in the middle, sits the father—providing ballast to this family scene and clearly enjoying his children's pleasure.

Steen has frozen the moment, sliced off a piece, and laid it on a canvas. He's told a story with a past, a present, and a future. These are real people in a real scene.

Steen's fun art reminds us that museums aren't mausoleums.

The Merry Family (1668)

This family—three generations living happily under one roof—is eating, drinking, and singing like there's no tomorrow. The broken eggshells and scattered cookware symbolize waste and extravagance. The neglected proverb tacked to the fireplace reminds us that children will follow in the

Steen's *Merry Family* may not be morally upright, but they sure know how to have fun.

footsteps of their parents. The father in this jolly scene is very drunk—ready to topple over—while in the foreground his mischievous daughter is feeding her brother wine straight from the flask. Mom and Grandma join the artist himself (playing the bagpipes) in a lively sing-along, but the child learning to smoke would rather follow Dad's lead.

Dutch Golden Age families were notoriously lenient with their kids. Even today, the Dutch describe a rowdy family as a "Jan Steen household."

Rembrandt van Rijn (1606-1669)

Rembrandt van Rijn is the greatest of all Dutch painters. Whereas most painters specialized in one field—portraits, landscapes, still lifes—Rembrandt excelled in them all.

The son of a Leiden miller who owned a waterwheel on the Rhine ("van Rijn"), Rembrandt took Amsterdam by storm with his famous painting of *The Anatomy Lesson* (1632, currently in The Hague). The commissions poured in for official portraits, and he was soon wealthy and married (1634) to Saskia van Uylenburgh. They moved to an expensive home in the

Jewish Quarter (today's Rembrandt's House museum—✪ see page 128), and decorated it with their collection of art and exotic furniture. His portraits were dutifully detailed, but other paintings explored strong contrasts of light and dark, with dramatic composition.

In 1642, Saskia died, and Rembrandt's fortunes changed, as the public's taste shifted and commissions dried up. In 1649, he hired an 18-year-old model named Hendrickje Stoffels, and she soon moved in with him and gave birth to their daughter.

Holland's war with England (1652-1654) devastated the art market, and Rembrandt's free-spending ways forced him to declare bankruptcy (1656)—the ultimate humiliation in success-oriented Amsterdam. The commissions came more slowly. The money ran out. His mother died. He had to auction off his paintings and furniture to pay debts. He moved out of his fine house to a cheaper place on Rozengracht. His bitter losses added a new wisdom to his work.

In his last years, his greatest works were his self-portraits, showing a tired, wrinkled man stoically enduring life's misfortunes. Rembrandt piled on layers of paint and glaze to capture increasingly subtle effects. In 1668, his lone surviving son, Titus, died, and Rembrandt passed away the next year. His death effectively marked the end of the Dutch Golden Age.

Isaac and Rebecca (a.k.a. *The Jewish Bride,* 1667)

The man gently draws the woman toward him. She's comfortable enough with him to sink into thought, and she reaches up unconsciously to return the gentle touch. They're young but wizened. This uncommissioned portrait (its subjects remain unknown) is a truly human look at the relationship between two people in love. They form a protective pyramid of love amid a gloomy background. The touching hands form the center of this somewhat sad but peaceful work. Van Gogh said that "Rembrandt alone has that tenderness—the heartbroken tenderness."

Rembrandt was a master of oil painting. In his later years, he rendered details with a messier, more Impressionistic style. The red-brown-gold of the couple's clothes is a patchwork of oil laid on thick with a palette knife.

The Syndics of the Amsterdam Drapers' Guild (*De Staalmeesters,* 1662)

Although commissions dwindled, Rembrandt could still paint an official group portrait better than anyone. In the painting made famous by Dutch

Rembrandt's tender *Jewish Bride*

The Night Watch—Civic Guards in action

Masters cigars, he catches the Drapers Guild in a natural but dignified pose (dignified, at least, until the guy on the left sits on his friend's lap).

It's a business meeting, and they're all dressed in black with black hats—the standard power suit of the Dutch Golden Age. They gather around a table examining the company's books. Suddenly, someone (us) walks in, and they look up. It's as natural as a snapshot, though X-rays show Rembrandt made many changes in posing them perfectly.

The figures are "framed" by the table beneath them and the top of the wood paneling above their heads, making a three-part composition that brings this band of colleagues together. Even in this simple portrait, we feel we can read the guild members' personalities in their faces. (If the table in the painting looks like it's sloping a bit unnaturally, lie on the floor to view it at Rembrandt's intended angle.)

▶ *At the far end of the Gallery of Honor stands the museum's star masterpiece. The best viewing spot is to the right of center—the angle Rembrandt had in mind when he designed it for its original location.*

The Night Watch (a.k.a. *The Company of Frans Banning Cocq,* 1642)

This is Rembrandt's most famous—though not necessarily greatest—painting. Created in 1642, when he was 36, it was one of his most important commissions: a group portrait of a company of Amsterdam's Civic Guards to hang in their meeting hall.

It's an action shot. With flags waving and drums beating, the guardsmen (who, by the 1640s, were really only an honorary militia of rich bigwigs) spill onto the street from under an arch in the back. It's "all for one and one for all" as they rush to Amsterdam's rescue. The soldiers grab lances and load their muskets. In the center, the commander (in black, with a red sash) strides forward energetically with a hand gesture that seems to say, "What are we waiting for? Let's move out!" His lieutenant focuses on his every order.

Rembrandt caught the optimistic spirit of Holland in the 1600s. Its war of independence from Spain was heading to victory and the economy was booming. These guardsmen on the move epitomize the proud, independent, upwardly mobile Dutch.

Why is *The Night Watch* so famous? Compare it with other, less famous group portraits, where every face is visible and everyone is well-lit, flat, and flashbulb-perfect. These people paid good money to have their mugs preserved for posterity, and they wanted it right up front. Other group portraits may be colorful, dignified works by a master...but not quite masterpieces.

By contrast, Rembrandt rousted the Civic Guards off their fat duffs. By adding movement and depth to an otherwise static scene, he took posers and turned them into warriors. He turned a simple portrait into great art.

OK, some *Night Watch* scuttlebutt: First off, *"Night Watch"* is a misnomer. It's a daytime scene, but over the years, as the preserving varnish darkened and layers of dirt built up, the sun set on this painting, and it got its popular title. When the painting was moved to a smaller room, the sides were lopped off (and the pieces lost), putting the two main characters in the center and causing the work to become more static than intended. During World War II, the painting was rolled up and hidden for five years. In 1975, a madman attacked the painting, slicing the captain's legs, and in 1990, it was sprayed with acid (it was skillfully restored after both incidents).

The Night Watch, contrary to popular myth, was a smashing success in its day. However, there are elements in it that show why Rembrandt soon fell out of favor as a portrait painter. He seemed to spend as much time painting the dwarf and the mysterious glowing girl with a chicken (the very appropriate mascot of this "militia" of shopkeepers) as he did the faces of his employers.

Rembrandt's life darkened long before his *Night Watch* did. This work marks the peak of Rembrandt's popularity...and the beginning of his fall from grace. He continued to paint masterpieces. Free from the dictates of employers whose taste was in their mouths, he painted what he wanted, how he wanted it. Rembrandt goes beyond mere craftsmanship to probe into, and draw life from, the deepest wells of the human soul.

▶ *Browse around the Grand Gallery and other second-floor rooms to find several other Rembrandt masterpieces.*

Self-Portrait at an Early Age (Young Rembrandt)

Here we see the young small-town boy about to launch himself into whatever life has to offer. Rembrandt was a precocious kid. His father, a miller, insisted that he become a lawyer. His mother hoped he'd be a preacher (look for a portrait of her reading the Bible). Rembrandt combined the secular and religious worlds by becoming an artist, someone who can hint at the spiritual by showing us the beauty of the created world.

Rembrandt moved to Amsterdam and entered the highly competitive art world. Amsterdam was a booming town and, like today, a hip and cosmopolitan city. Rembrandt portrays himself at age 22 as being divided—half in light, half hidden by hair and shadows—open-eyed, but wary of an uncertain future. As we'll see, Rembrandt's paintings are often light and dark, both in color and in subject, exploring the "darker" side of human experience.

Jeremiah Lamenting the Destruction of Jerusalem (1630)

The Babylonians have sacked and burned Jerusalem, but Rembrandt leaves the pyrotechnics (in the murky background at left) to Spielberg and the big screen. Instead, he tells the story of Israel's destruction in the face of the prophet who predicted the disaster. Jeremiah slumps in defeat, deep in thought, confused and despondent, trying to understand why this

Young Rembrandt—what does his future hold?

Jeremiah—brooding in the darkness

evil had to happen. Rembrandt turns his floodlight of truth on the prophet's deeply lined forehead.

Rembrandt wasn't satisfied to crank out portraits of fat merchants in frilly bibs, no matter what they paid him. He wanted to experiment, trying new techniques and more probing subjects. Many of his paintings weren't commissioned and were never even intended for sale. His subjects could be brooding and melancholy, a bit dark for the public's taste. His technique set him apart—you can recognize a Rembrandt canvas by his play of light and dark. Most of his paintings are a deep brown tone, with only a few bright spots glowing from the darkness. This allows Rembrandt to highlight the details he thinks are most important and to express moody emotions.

Maria Trip (1639)

This debutante daughter of a wealthy citizen is shy and reserved—maybe a bit awkward in her new dress and adult role, but still self-assured. When he chose to, Rembrandt could dash off a commissioned portrait like nobody's business. The details are immaculate—the lace and shiny satin, the pearls behind the veil, the subtle face and hands. Rembrandt gives us not just a person, but a personality.

Look at the red rings around her eyes, a detail a lesser painter would have airbrushed out. Rembrandt takes this feature, unique to her, and uses it as a setting for her luminous, jewel-like eyes. Without being prettified, she's beautiful.

A Young Woman (a.k.a. The Portrait of Saskia, 1633)

As Rembrandt became known in Amsterdam, everyone wanted a portrait done by the young master, and he became wealthy and famous. He fell in love with and married the rich, beautiful, and cultured Saskia. By all accounts, the two were enormously happy, entertaining friends, decorating their house with fine furniture, raising a family, and living the high life. In this wedding portrait, thought to be of Saskia, the bride's face literally glows. A dash of white paint puts a sparkle in her eye. Barely 30 years old, Rembrandt was the most successful painter in Holland. He had it all.

Self-Portrait as the Apostle Paul (1661)

Rembrandt's many self-portraits show us the evolution of a great painter's

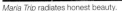
Maria Trip radiates honest beauty.

Self-portrait: These eyes have seen it all.

style, as well as the progress of a genius's life. For Rembrandt, the two were intertwined.

Compare this later self-portrait (he's 55 but looks 70) with the youthful, curious Rembrandt of age 22 we saw earlier. With a lined forehead, a bulbous nose, and messy hair, he peers out from under several coats of glazing, holding old, wrinkled pages. His look is...skeptical? Weary? Resigned to life's misfortunes? Or amused? (He's looking at us, but not *just* at us—remember that a self-portrait is done staring into a mirror.)

This man has seen it all—success, love, money, fatherhood, loss, poverty, death. He took these experiences and wove them into his art. Rembrandt died poor and misunderstood, but he remained very much his own man to the end.

▶ *Wander through both sides of the second-floor galleries to see other 17th-century masterpieces.*

Bartholomeus Van der Helst's glorious group portrait is just one of many Golden Age treasures.

Still life—the beauty of everyday things

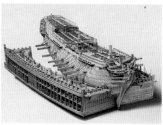

The Rijks remembers the rich Golden Age.

More Golden Age Treasures

Welcome to the Dutch Golden Age. As you browse the rest of the second floor, look for...

Group Portraits: These men helped make Amsterdam the richest city on earth in the 1600s. Though shown in their military uniforms, these men were really captains of industry—shipbuilders, seamen, salesmen, spice-tasters, bankers, and venture capitalists—all part of the complex economic web that planned and financed overseas trade.

Still Lifes: Savor the fruits of Holland's rich overseas trade—lemons from the south, pewterware from Germany, and spices from Asia. Pick a still life, and get so close that the guard joins you. Linger over the little things. You'd swear you could see yourself reflected in the pewter vessels. The closer you get, the better it looks. These carefully composed, photo-realistic still lifes reflect the same sense of pride the Dutch have for their homes, cultivating them like gardens until they're immaculate, decorative, and in perfect order.

Artifacts: You'll see everyday items such as dolls' houses *(poppen-huizen),* a ship's cannon, or a big wooden model of a 74-gun Dutch man-of-war that had escorted convoys of merchant ships loaded with wealth.

The Rest of the Rijks

Most visitors are here to see the Golden Age art, but the museum has much, much more, with upward of 8,000 works on display—including a Van Gogh self-portrait (on the first floor), an airplane (third floor), women's fashion and delftware (Level 0), and art from Indonesia, a former Dutch colony (Level 0).

Linger over these objects, appreciating the beauty of everyday things.

Van Gogh Museum Tour

The Van Gogh Museum (we say "van GO," the Dutch say "van HHHOCK") is a cultural high even for those not into art. Located near the Rijksmuseum, the museum houses the 200 paintings owned by Vincent's younger brother, Theo. It's a user-friendly stroll through the work and life of one enigmatic man. If you like brightly colored landscapes in the Impressionist style, you'll like this museum. If you enjoy finding deeper meaning in works of art, you'll really love it. The mix of Van Gogh's creative genius, his tumultuous life, and the traveler's determination to connect to it makes this museum as much a walk with Vincent as with his art.

ORIENTATION

Cost: €15, more for special exhibits. Credit cards accepted (€25 minimum).

Hours: Daily 9:00-17:00, Fri until 22:00, closed Jan 1.

Avoiding Lines: Skip the 15- to 30-minute wait in the ticket-buying line with a Museumkaart or I amsterdam Card, or buy advance tickets at a TI or online at vangoghmuseum.nl. Friday evenings are least crowded and have a relaxed atmosphere (wine bar, DJ).

Getting There: It's a few blocks behind the Rijksmuseum at Paulus Potterstraat 7. From Central Station, catch tram #2 or #5 to Hobbemastraat.

Information: Free floor plan with brief history of Vincent's life. A 15-minute video introduction plays continuously in the downstairs auditorium. The popular bookstore sells good guidebooks and posters (with mailing tubes). Tel. 020/570-5200, vangoghmuseum.nl.

Audioguide: The €5 audioguide includes 90 creatively produced minutes of insightful commentaries about Van Gogh's paintings, along with related quotations from Vincent himself.

Length of This Tour: Allow one hour.

Baggage Check: Free and mandatory.

Cuisine Art: The museum café (€10 plates, €6 salads, €4 sandwiches) is OK.

Photography: No photos allowed.

The Van Gogh Museum on Museumplein

Avoid crowds by visiting on Friday evening.

THE TOUR BEGINS

Climb the stairs to the first floor. The core of the museum (and this entire tour) is on the first floor. The paintings are arranged chronologically, divided into five periods of Vincent's life. The first room—often displaying self-portraits—introduces you to the artist.

Vincent van Gogh (1853-1890)

I am a man of passions... —Vincent van Gogh

You could see Vincent van Gogh's canvases as a series of suicide notes—or as the record of a life full of beauty...perhaps too full of beauty. He attacked life with a passion, experiencing highs and lows more intensely than the average person. The beauty of the world overwhelmed him; its ugliness struck him as only another dimension of beauty. He tried to absorb the full

Self-portraits chronicle the stages of Vincent's life—his youth in Holland, Paris, Provence.

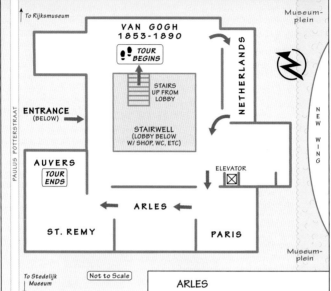

Van Gogh Museum—2nd Floor

To Rijksmuseum

Museum-plein

VAN GOGH
1853-1890

TOUR BEGINS

STAIRS UP FROM LOBBY

NETHERLANDS

NEW WING

ENTRANCE (BELOW)

STAIRWELL
(LOBBY BELOW W/ SHOP, WC, ETC)

PAULUS POTTERSTRAAT

AUVERS
TOUR ENDS

ELEVATOR

ARLES

ST. REMY

PARIS

Museum-plein

To Stedelijk Museum

Not to Scale

NETHERLANDS
The Potato Eaters
Still Life with Bible
The Old Church Tower at Nuenen

PARIS
Self-Portrait as an Artist
Self-Portrait with Straw Hat
Cabbages and Onions
Self-Portrait with Gray Felt Hat

ARLES
The Yellow House
Sunflowers
The Bedroom
Gauguin's Chair
The Sower

ST. REMY / AUVERS-sur-OISE
Pietà
The Garden of Saint Paul's Hospital
Wheatfield with a Reaper
The Sheaf-Binder
Almond Blossom
Wheatfield with Crows

spectrum of experience, good and bad, and channel it onto a canvas. The frustration of this overwhelming task drove him to madness. If all this is a bit overstated—and I guess it is—it's an attempt to show the emotional impact that Van Gogh's works have had on many people, me included.

Vincent, a pastor's son from a small Dutch town, started working at age 16 as a clerk for an art dealership. But his two interests, art and religion, distracted him from his dreary work, and after several years, he was fired.

The next 10 years were a collage of dead ends as he traveled northern Europe pursuing one path after another. He launched into each project with incredible energy, then became disillusioned and moved on to something else: teacher at a boarding school, assistant preacher, bookstore apprentice, preacher again, theology student, English student, literature student, art student. He bounced around England, France, Belgium, and the Netherlands. He fell in love, but was rejected for someone more respectable. He quarreled with his family and was estranged. He lived with a prostitute and her daughter, offending the few friends he had. Finally, in his late 20s, worn out, flat broke, and in poor health, he returned to his family in Nuenen and made peace. He then started to paint.

▶ *For his stark early work, enter the next room.*

The Netherlands (1880-1885): Poverty and Religion

These dark, gray canvases show us the hard, plain existence of the people and town of Nuenen, in the rural southern Netherlands. We see simple buildings, bare or autumnal trees, and overcast skies—a world where it seems spring will never arrive. What warmth there is comes from the sturdy, gentle people themselves.

The style is crude—Van Gogh couldn't draw very well and would never become a great technician. The paint is laid on thick, as though painted with Nuenen mud. The main subject is almost always dead center, with little or no background, so there's a claustrophobic feeling. We are unable to see anything but the immediate surroundings.

The Potato Eaters (1885)

Those that prefer to see the peasants in their Sunday-best may do as they like. I personally am convinced I get better results by painting them in their roughness...If a peasant picture smells of bacon, smoke, potato steam—all right, that's healthy. —Vincent van Gogh

Potato Eaters—the peasants he worked with

Still Life with Bible—son of a minister

In a dark, cramped room lit only by a dim lamp, poor workers help themselves to a steaming plate of potatoes. They've earned it. Vincent deliberately wanted the canvas to be potato-colored.

Vincent had dabbled as an artist during his wandering years, sketching things around him and taking a few art classes, but it wasn't until age 29 that he painted his first oil canvas. He soon threw himself into it with abandon.

He painted the poor working peasants. He worked as a lay minister among the poorest of the poor, peasants and miners. He joined them at work in the mines, taught their children, and even gave away his own few possessions to help them. The church authorities finally dismissed him for "excessive zeal," but he came away understanding the poor's harsh existence and the dignity with which they bore it.

Still Life with Bible (1885)

I have a terrible need of—shall I say the word?—religion. Then I go out and paint the stars. —Vincent van Gogh

The Bible and Emile Zola's *La Joie de Vivre*—these two books dominated Van Gogh's life. In his art he tried to fuse his religious upbringing with his love of the world's beauty. He lusted after life with a religious fervor. The burned-out candle tells us of the recent death of his father. The Bible is open to Isaiah 53: "He was despised and rejected of men, a man of sorrows..."

The Old Church Tower at Nuenen (1885)

The crows circle above the local cemetery of Nuenen. Soon after his father's death, Vincent—in poor health and depressed—moved briefly to

Antwerp. He then decided to visit his brother Theo, an art dealer living in Paris, the art capital of the world. Theo's support—financial and emotional—allowed Vincent to spend the rest of his short life painting.

Vincent moved from rural, religious, poor Holland to Paris, the City of Light. Vincent van Gone.

▶ *Continue to...*

Paris (March 1886-Feb 1888): Impressionism

The sun begins to break through, lighting up everything Van Gogh paints. His canvases are more colorful and the landscapes more spacious, with plenty of open sky, giving a feeling of exhilaration after the closed, dark world of Nuenen.

In the cafés and bars of Paris' bohemian Montmartre district, Vincent met the revolutionary Impressionists. He roomed with Theo and became friends with other struggling young painters, such as Paul Gauguin and Henri de Toulouse-Lautrec. His health improved. He became more sociable, had an affair with an older woman, and was generally happy.

He signed up to study under a well-known classical teacher but quit after only a few classes. He couldn't afford to hire models, so he roamed the streets, sketch pad in hand, and learned from his Impressionist friends.

The Impressionists emphasized getting out of the stuffy studio and setting up canvases outside on the street or in the countryside to paint the play of sunlight off the trees, buildings, and water.

As you see in this room, at first, Vincent copied from the Impressionist masters. He painted garden scenes like Claude Monet, café snapshots like Edgar Degas, "block prints" like the Japanese masters, and self-portraits like...nobody else.

Church Tower, Nuenen—dark hometown scene

In Paris, the artist found bright colors.

Self-Portrait as an Artist (1888)

I am now living with my brother Vincent, who is studying the art of painting with indefatigable zeal. —Theo van Gogh to a friend

Here, the budding young artist proudly displays his new palette full of bright new colors, trying his hand at the Impressionist technique of building a scene using dabs of different-colored paint. A whole new world of art—and life—opened up to him in Paris.

Self-Portrait with Straw Hat (1887)

You wouldn't recognize Vincent, he has changed so much.... The doctor says that he is now perfectly fit again. He is making tremendous strides with his work.... He is also far livelier than he used to be and is popular with people. —Theo van Gogh to their mother

Vincent's vibrant self-portraits capture his restless energy. The shimmering effect is created by placing brushstrokes of different colors side by side on the canvas. At a distance, the two colors blend in the eye of the viewer to become a third color. Here, Vincent uses separate strokes of blue, yellow, green, and red to create a brown beard—but a brown that throbs with excitement.

Still Lifes, such as *Cabbages and Onions* (1887)

Vincent quickly developed his own style: thicker paint; broad, swirling brushstrokes; and brighter, clashing colors that make even inanimate objects seem to pulsate with life. The many different colors are supposed to blend together, but you'd have to back up to Belgium to make these colors resolve into focus.

With straw hat and pipe, he painted outdoors.

Traditional still life with modern colors

Thick brushstrokes radiate outward, magnifying the artist's ultra-intense gaze.

Self-Portrait with Gray Felt Hat (1887-1888)

He has painted one or two portraits which have turned out well, but he insists on working for nothing. It is a pity that he shows no desire to earn some money because he could easily do so here. But you can't change people. —Theo van Gogh to their mother

Despite his new sociability, Vincent never quite fit in with his Impressionist friends. As he developed into a good painter, he became anxious to strike out on his own. Also, he thought the social life of the big city was distracting him from serious work. In this painting, his face screams out from a swirling background of molecular activity. He wanted peace and quiet, a place where he could throw himself into his work completely. He headed for the sunny south of France.

▶ *Travel to the next room to reach...*

Arles (Feb 1888-May 1889): Sunlight, Beauty, and Madness
Winter was just turning to spring when Vincent arrived in Arles, near the French Riviera. After the dreary Paris winter, the colors of springtime overwhelmed him. The blossoming trees inspired him to paint canvas after canvas, drenched in sunlight.

The Yellow House (a.k.a. The Street, 1888)
It is my intention...to go temporarily to the South, where there is even more color, even more sun. —Vincent van Gogh

Vincent rented this house with the green shutters. (He ate at the pink café next door.) Look at that blue sky! He painted in a frenzy, working feverishly to try and take it all in. For the next nine months, he produced an explosion of canvases, working very quickly when the mood possessed him. His unique style evolved beyond the Impressionists'—thicker paint, stronger outlines, brighter colors (often applied right from the paint tube), and swirling brushwork that makes inanimate objects pulse and vibrate with life.

Sunflowers (1889)
The worse I get along with people, the more I learn to have faith in Nature and concentrate on her. —Vincent van Gogh

His *Yellow House* in sunny Arles

His bedroom, fit for the monastic artist

Vincent saw sunflowers as his signature subject, and he painted a half-dozen versions of them, each a study in intense yellow. If he signed the work (look on the vase), it means he was proud of it.

Even a simple work like these sunflowers bursts with life. Different people see different things in *Sunflowers*. Is it a happy painting, or is it a melancholy one? Take your own emotional temperature and see.

The Bedroom (1888)

I am a man of passions, capable of and subject to doing more or less foolish things—which I happen to regret, more or less, afterwards. —Vincent van Gogh

Vincent was alone, a Dutchman in Provence. And that had its downside. He swung from flurries of ecstatic activity to bouts of great loneliness. Like anyone traveling alone, he experienced those high highs and low lows. This narrow, trapezoid-shaped, single-room apartment (less than 200 square feet) must have seemed like a prison cell at times. (Psychologists have pointed out that most everything in this painting comes in pairs—two chairs, two paintings, a double bed squeezed down to a single—indicating his desire for a mate. Hmm.)

He invited his friend Paul Gauguin to join him, envisioning a sort of artists' colony in Arles. He spent months preparing a room upstairs for Gauguin's arrival.

Gauguin's Chair (1888)

Empty chairs—there are many of them, there will be even more, and sooner or later, there will be nothing but empty chairs. —Vincent van Gogh

Gauguin arrived. At first, they got along great, painting and carousing. But then things went sour. They clashed over art, life, and personalities. On Christmas Eve 1888, Vincent went ballistic. Enraged during an alcohol-fueled argument, he pulled out a knife and waved it in Gauguin's face. Gauguin took the hint and quickly left town. Vincent was horrified at himself. In a fit of remorse and madness, he mutilated his own ear and presented it to a prostitute.

The Sower (1888)

A dark, silhouetted figure sows seeds in the burning sun. It's late in the day. The heat from the sun, the source of all life, radiates out in thick swirls of paint. The sower must be a hopeful man, because the field looks slanted

Gauguin's Chair: When his friend visited, Vincent drove him away in a fit of madness.

and barren. Someday, he thinks, the seeds he's planting will grow into something great, like the tree that slashes diagonally across the scene—tough and craggy, but with small, optimistic blossoms.

In his younger years, Vincent had worked in Belgium sowing the Christian gospel in a harsh environment (see Mark 4:1-9). Now in Arles, ignited by the sun, he cast his artistic seeds to the wind, hoping.

▸ *Continue into the next room. Paintings featured in the rest of this tour are shifted around a lot, so they'll likely be in a different order than listed here.*

St. Rémy (May 1889-1890): The Mental Hospital

The people of Arles realized they had a madman on their hands. A doctor diagnosed "acute mania with hallucinations," and the local vicar talked Vincent into admitting himself to a mental hospital. Vincent wrote to Theo: "Temporarily I wish to remain shut up, as much for my own peace of mind as for other people's."

In the mental hospital, Vincent continued to paint whenever he was well enough. He often couldn't go out, so he copied from books, making his own distinctive versions of works by Rembrandt, Delacroix, Millet, and others.

We see a change from bright, happy landscapes to more introspective subjects. The colors are less bright and more surreal, the brushwork even more furious. The strong outlines of figures are twisted and tortured.

Pietà, after Delacroix (1889)

It's evening after a thunderstorm. Jesus has been crucified, and the corpse lies at the mouth of a tomb. Mary, whipped by the cold wind, holds her empty arms out in despair and confusion. She is the tender mother who receives us all in death, as though saying, "My child, you've been away so long—rest in my arms." Christ has a Vincent-esque red beard.

At first, the peace and quiet of the asylum did Vincent good, and his health improved. Occasionally, he was allowed outside to paint the gardens and landscapes. Meanwhile, the paintings he had sent to Theo began to attract attention in Paris for the first time. A woman in Brussels bought one of his canvases—the only painting he ever sold during his lifetime. In 1987, one of his *Sunflowers* sold for $40 million. Three years later a portrait of Vincent's doctor went for more than $80 million.

This *Pietà* creates a mystical mood.

The trees ripple with an inner force.

The Garden of Saint Paul's Hospital (a.k.a. *The Fall of the Leaves*, 1889)

...a traveler going to a destination that does not exist... —Vincent van Gogh

The stark brown trees are blown by the wind. A solitary figure (Vincent?) winds along a narrow, snaky path as the wind blows leaves on him. The colors are surreal—blue, green, and red tree trunks with heavy black outlines. A road runs away from us, heading nowhere.

Wheatfield with a Reaper (1889)

I have been working hard and fast in the last few days. This is how I try to express how desperately fast things pass in modern life. —Vincent van Gogh

The harvest is here. The time is short. There's much work to be done. A lone reaper works uphill, scything through a swirling wheat field, cutting slender paths of calm.

The Sheaf-Binder, after Millet (1889)

I want to paint men and women with that something of the eternal which the halo used to symbolize... —Vincent van Gogh

Vincent's compassion for honest laborers remained constant. These sturdy folk, with their curving bodies, wrestle as one with their curving wheat. The world Vincent sees is charged from within by spiritual fires, twisting and turning matter into energy, and vice versa.

The fits of madness returned. During these spells, he lost all sense of his own actions. He couldn't paint, the one thing he felt driven to do. He wrote to Theo, "My surroundings here begin to weigh on me more than I can say—I need air. I feel overwhelmed by boredom and grief."

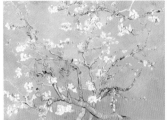

Vincent portrays workers with noble dignity.

The fleeting glory of the *Almond Blossom*

Auvers-sur-Oise (May-July 1890): Flying Away

The bird looks through the bars at the overcast sky where a thunderstorm is gathering, and inwardly he rebels against his fate. 'I am caged, I am caged, and you tell me I have everything I need! Oh! I beg you, give me liberty, that I may be a bird like other birds.' A certain idle man resembles this idle bird...
—Vincent van Gogh

Almond Blossom (1890)

Vincent moved north to Auvers, a small town near Paris where he could stay at a hotel under a doctor friend's supervision. On the way there, he visited Theo. Theo's wife had just had a baby, whom they named Vincent. Brother Vincent showed up with this painting under his arm as a birthday gift. Theo's wife later recalled, "I had expected a sick man, but here was a sturdy, broad-shouldered man with a healthy color, a smile on his face, and a very resolute appearance."

In his new surroundings, he continued painting, averaging a canvas a day, but was interrupted by spells that swung from boredom to madness. His letters to Theo were generally optimistic, but he worried that he'd soon succumb completely to insanity and never paint again. The final landscapes are walls of bright, thick paint.

Wheatfield with Crows (1890)

This new attack...came on me in the fields, on a windy day, when I was busy painting. —Vincent van Gogh

On July 27, 1890, Vincent left his hotel, walked out to a nearby field, and put a bullet through his chest.

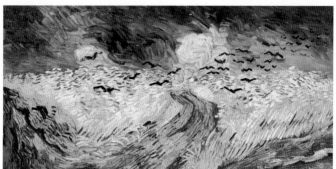

Vincent's last painting, of a field like the one where he would end his short life

This is the last painting Vincent finished. We can try to search the wreckage of his life for the black box explaining what happened, but there's not much there. His life was sad and tragic, but the record he left is one not of sadness, but of beauty—intense beauty.

The windblown wheat field is a nest of restless energy. Scenes like this must have overwhelmed Vincent with their incredible beauty—too much, too fast, with no release. The sky is stormy and dark blue, almost nighttime, barely lit by two suns boiling through the deep ocean of blue. The road starts nowhere, leads nowhere, disappearing into the burning wheat field. Above all of this swirling beauty fly the crows, the dark ghosts that had hovered over his life since the cemetery in Nuenen.

The Rest of the Museum

The ground floor displays paintings by artists who preceded and influenced Van Gogh's generation. The second floor has a study area and more paintings (including Van Gogh's smaller-scale works). The third floor shows works by his friends and colleagues—Monet, Gauguin, Toulouse-Lautrec, etc. The exhibition wing in the basement showcases temporary exhibitions.

Red Light District Walk

Amsterdam's oldest neighborhood has hosted the world's oldest profession since the Middle Ages. Today, prostitution still thrives here, creating a spectacle that's unique in all of Europe.

On our walk, we'll see history, sleaze, and cheese: transvestites in windows, drunks in doorways, and cannabis in bongs. The main event is prostitution: ladies in bras, thongs, and high heels, standing in window displays, offering their bodies—and it's all legal.

Not for Everyone: The Red Light District seems to have something to offend everyone. Whether it's in-your-face images of graphic sex, exploited immigrant women, whips and chains, the pungent smells of pot and urine, or just the shameless commercialism of it all, it's not everyone's cup of tea. And though I encourage people to expand their horizons, it's perfectly OK to say, "No, thank you."

ORIENTATION

Length of This Walk: Allow two hours.

When to Go: Evenings (16:00-22:30) are lively with tourists, safe, and festive. Mornings are dead, and late night gets creepy.

Photography: Taking any photos of ladies in windows is absolutely forbidden, and will instantly unleash a snarling bouncer. Photos of historic landmarks are OK, but remember that a camera or phone is a prime target in this high-theft area.

Safety: There are plenty of police, but also plenty of rowdy drunks, drug-pushing lowlifes, con artists, and pickpockets. Stay alert. Assume any fight or commotion is a ploy to allow pickpockets to prey on distracted bystanders.

Old Church (Oude Kerk): Interior-€5, more for temporary exhibits, Mon-Sat 11:00-17:00, Sun 13:00-17:00. Tower climb-€7, April-Sept Thu-Sat 13:00-17:00, closed Sun-Wed and off-season.

Prostitution Information Center: €1, Sat 13:30-20:00 only, tel. 020/420-7328, pic-amsterdam.com.

Amstelkring Museum (Our Lord in the Attic): €8, Mon-Sat 10:00-17:00, Sun and holidays 13:00-17:00, no photos.

Cannabis College: Free, daily 11:00-19:00.

Hash, Marijuana, and Hemp Museum: €9 (includes nearby Hemp Gallery), daily 10:00-23:00.

Audio Tour: You can download this chapter as a free Rick Steves audio tour (✪ see page 167).

THE WALK BEGINS

▶ *Start on Dam Square. Face the big, fancy Grand Hotel Krasnapolsky. To the left of the hotel stretches the long street called...*

❶ Warmoesstraat

As you walk down Warmoesstraat, you're walking along one of the city's oldest streets—the traditional border of the neighborhood tourists call the Red Light District.

Amsterdammers call the area De Wallen, or "The Walls," after the old retaining walls that once stood here. De Wallen is the oldest part of

Condom shop—be prepared.

Smartshops sell natural hallucinogens.

town, with the oldest church. It grew up between the harbor and the Dam Square, where the city was born. A port town, Amsterdam traded in all kinds of goods, including things popular with sailors and businessmen away from home—like sex and drugs. The sex trade has been plied here since the 1200s. For centuries, it existed alongside everyday life. Then, in the 1980s, the city designated De Wallen as the neighborhood where prostitution could be legally conducted.

You'll pass the **Golden Fleece Condomerie** (Het Gulden Vlies, at #141), a condom store with a flair. Located at the entrance to the Red Light District, this is the perfect place to get prepared.

Continue down Warmoesstraat. The two little street barricades **(bollards),** with cute red lights around them, mark the official entrance to the traffic-free world of De Wallen.

According to legend, Quentin Tarantino holed up at the **Winston Hotel** (at #129) for three months in 1993 to write *Pulp Fiction*.

Notice all the **Irish pubs,** advertisements for football (soccer) games, and foreign flags. For Brits, Amsterdam is just a cheap flight away—perfect for a weekend getaway or stag party.

The small cross-street called **Wijde Kerksteeg** leads to the Old Church.

If you were to continue on Warmoesstraat, you'd come to **Elements of Nature** (at #97) "smartshop." These clean, well-lit, fully professional retail outlets sell powerful drugs, many of which are illegal in America. Because the drugs are "natural," the Dutch consider them beyond the reach of the law.

Smartshops sell everything from harmless nutrition boosters (such as royal jelly), to tobacco, herbal versions of popular dance-club drugs like

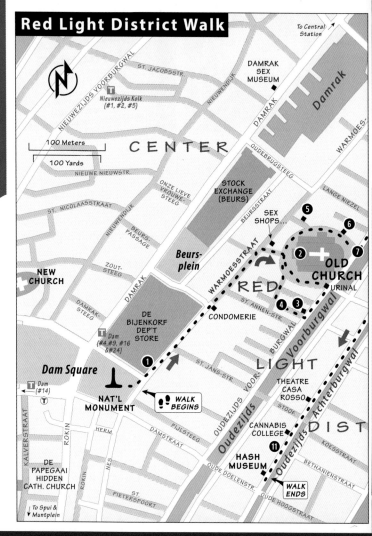

Red Light District Walk

To Central Station

DAMRAK SEX MUSEUM

Damrak

NIEUWEZIJDS VOORBURGWAL

ST. JACOBSSTR.

NIEUWENDIJK

Nieuwezijds Kolk (#1, #2, #5)

CENTER

OUDEBRUGSTEEG

WARMOES-

BEURSSTRAAT

STOCK EXCHANGE (BEURS)

LANGE NIEZEL

SEX SHOPS...

⑤

⑥

② ✚ OLD CHURCH ⑦

NIEUWE NIEUWSTR.

ONZE LIEVE VROUWE-STEEG

ST. NICOLAASSTRAAT

NIEUWENDIJK

BEURS-PASSAGE

Beurs-plein

WARMOESSTRAAT

RED

URINAL

ZOUT-STEEG

NEW CHURCH

DAMRAK

Beursplein

ST. ANNEN-STR.

④ ③

CONDOMERIE

BURGWAL

Voorburgwal

DAMRAK-STEEG

DE BIJENKORF DEP'T STORE

Dam (#4,#9, #16 &#24)

①

ST. JANS-STR.

LIGHT

Achterburgwal

Dam Square

NAT'L MONUMENT

👣 WALK BEGINS

Oudezijds Voor-

THEATRE CASA ROSSO

DIST

Dam (#14)

KALVERSTRAAT

ROKIN

HERM.

DAMSTRAAT

PIJLSTEEG

STOOF

CANNABIS COLLEGE

Oudezijds

KOESGRACHT

DE PAPEGAAI HIDDEN CATH. CHURCH

ROKIN

NES

ST. PIETERSPOORT

⑪

HASH MUSEUM

WALK ENDS

BETHANIENSTRAAT

To Spui & Muntplein

OUDE DOELENSTR.

OUDE HOOGSTRAAT

100 Meters

100 Yards

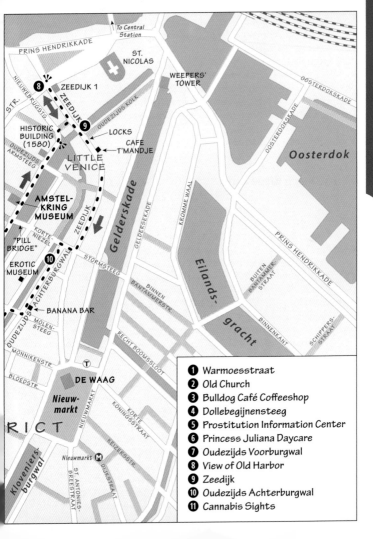

To Central Station

PRINS HENDRIKKADE

ST. NICOLAS

WEEPERS' TOWER

OOSTERDOKSKADE

8 ZEEDIJK 1

NIEUWEBRUGSTG.

STR.

ZEEDIJK

OUDEZIJDS KOLK

OOSTERDOKSKADE

HISTORIC BUILDING (1580)

9 LOCKS

CAFE T'MANDJE

Oosterdok

OUDEZIJDS ARMSTEEG

LITTLE VENICE

AMSTEL-KRING MUSEUM

ZEEDIJK

GELDERSKADE

K'ROMME WAAL

PRINS HENDRIKKADE

KORTE NIEZEL

"PILL BRIDGE"

10 STORMSTEEG

ACHTERBURGWAL

BINNEN BANTAMNERSTR.

Eilands-

BUITEN BANTAMMER-STRAAT

EROTIC MUSEUM

BINNENKANT

SCHIPPERS-STRAAT

BANANA BAR

OUDEZIJDS MOLEN-STEEG

RECHT BOOMSSLOOT

gracht

MONNIKENSTR.

BLOEDSTR.

DE WAAG

Nieuw-markt

NIEUWMARKT

KORTE KONINGSSTRAAT

RICT

Nieuwmarkt Ⓜ

KEIZERSSTR.

Kloveniers-burgwal

ST. ANTONIES-BREESTRAAT

DIJKSTRAAT

❶ Warmoesstraat
❷ Old Church
❸ Bulldog Café Coffeeshop
❹ Dollebegijnensteeg
❺ Prostitution Information Center
❻ Princess Juliana Daycare
❼ Oudezijds Voorburgwal
❽ View of Old Harbor
❾ Zeedijk
❿ Oudezijds Achterburgwal
⓫ Cannabis Sights

Ecstasy, marijuana seeds, and hallucinogenic truffles. Prices are clearly marked, with descriptions of the drugs and their effects. The knowledgeable salespeople can give you more information on their "100 percent natural products that play with the human senses."

Farther down Warmoesstraat, you'd find a number of **sex shops** selling various erotic paraphernalia—dildos, S&M starter kits, and kinky magazines and videos. While Amsterdam is notorious for its Red Light District, even small Dutch towns often have a sex shop and a brothel to satisfy their citizens' needs.

▶ *But for now, let's go see the Old Church. Head down Wijde Kerksteeg to the...*

② Old Church (Oude Kerk)

As the name implies, this was the medieval city's original church. Returning from a long sea voyage, sailors of yore would spy the steeple of the Old Church on the horizon and know they were home. Having returned safely, they'd come here to give thanks to St. Nicholas—the patron saint of this church, of seafarers, of Christmas, and of the city of Amsterdam.

The church was begun about 1300. Construction continued in fits and starts for the next 300 years—as is apparent in the building's many gangly parts. Then, in the 15th century, Amsterdam built the New Church (Nieuwe Kerk) on Dam Square. But the Old Church still had the tallest spire and biggest organ, and it remained the city's center of activity, bustling inside and out with merchants and street markets.

The **tower** is 290 feet high, with an octagonal steeple atop a bell tower (you can pay to climb to the top). This tower served as the model for many other Dutch steeples. The carillon has 47 bells, which can chime mechanically or be played by one of Amsterdam's three official carillonneurs.

While the church is historic, there's not much to see inside. If you pay to enter, you'll see a big empty church with 2,500 gravestones in the floor. The most famous grave is that of Rembrandt's wife, Saskia.

Nowadays, the church is the holy needle around which the unholy Red Light District spins. This marks the neighborhood's most dense concentration of prostitution.

Back outside, explore around the right side of the church. You'll see a statue, dedicated to the Unknown Prostitute. Attached to the church like barnacles are small buildings. These were originally used as homes for priests, church offices, or rental units. The house to the right of the

Old Church—historic charm amid the sleaze

Statue honoring the Unknown Prostitute

entrance (at #25) is very tiny—32 feet by 8 feet. (Elderly people live here, so be discreet.)

Now check out the green metal **urinal** over by the canal. This one gets a lot of use.

▶ *From the urinal, go half a block south along the canal toward the...*

❸ Bulldog Café Coffeeshop

The Bulldog claims to be Amsterdam's very first marijuana coffeeshop, established here in 1975. Now there's a chain of Bulldogs around the city. At "coffeeshops" like this one, customers start the transaction by asking the bartender, "Can I see the cannabis menu?" Then the bartender pulls out a display case with different varieties of weed, sold in baggies or pre-rolled joints. It's all clearly priced, and available either to-go or to smoke on the premises. You'll see people at the Bulldog enjoying a joint while they sip a beer or a Coke.

As coffeeshops go, the Bulldog is considered pretty touristy, meant for young foreigners. Connoisseurs prefer smaller places with better-quality pot and a mellower ambience.

In recent years, various Dutch politicians have proposed new laws that would forbid sales of marijuana to nonresidents. But many Amsterdam businesses depend on out-of-town stoners for their livelihood.

▶ *Time to dive into the heart of the Red Light District—the world of legal prostitution. Immediately adjacent to the coffeeshop is a three-foot-wide entrance to a narrow alleyway called Dollebegijnensteeg.*

At the far end of the alleyway is a T-intersection, where—if things get too hairy—you can turn right to return to the Old Church. Got it? Now

Marijuana coffeeshop—no big deal here   Narrow alley with prostitutes in windows

take a deep breath, set your sights on those red lights, and let's plunge ahead.

❹ Dollebegijnensteeg

You're right in the thick of high-density prostitution. Remember: Don't take any pictures, and watch for pickpockets if crowds jostle together. If you do both these things, you'll be fine.

As you pass window after window of women in panties and bras, notice how they wink at the horny men, rap on the window to attract attention, or look disdainfully at sightseers. You can take your time here and then explore deeper (or you can hurry to the end of the block and turn right to return to the Old Church).

This alleyway is just one of several in this area. You may notice that different zones feature prostitutes from different lands—Asia, Africa, Eastern Europe. This is to cater to customer tastes, as regulars know what they want.

▶ *Return to the Old Church and start to circle the church clockwise. Around the back (on Oudekerksplein), you'll see older, plumper (and cheaper) prostitutes. In the same area, at Enge Kerksteeg 3, is the...*

❺ Prostitution Information Center (PIC)

This center exists solely to demystify prostitution, giving visitors matter-of-fact information on how the trade works and what it's like to be a sex worker. It's only open on Saturday evenings, when it doles out pamphlets, books, condoms, T-shirts, and other offbeat souvenirs.

Next door is a **room-rental office** (labeled *Kamerverhuurbedrijf*). Prostitutes come here to rent window space and bedrooms to use for their

Red Light areas have strict security video.

The "PIC" has info about the sex trade.

work. Several of the available rooms for rent are just next door. The office also sells supplies—condoms by the case, lubricants, and soft drinks. The man at the desk does not arrange sex. The women who rent space from this business are self-employed, and negotiate directly with their customers.

In return for their rental fees, prostitutes get security. The man in the office keeps an eye on them by video surveillance—you can see the monitors inside. Looking down the street, you can see small cameras and orange alarm lights above the doors. If prostitutes have any trouble, they press a buzzer that swiftly unleashes not a pimp, but a burly bouncer or the police. The area sure looks rough, but, aside from tricky pickpockets, these streets are actually pretty safe.

▶ *Continue circling clockwise around the church. Amid prostitutes in windows, find the orange brick building on the left at Oudekerksplein 8. (Because it's low-profile and sealed up tight, it might be hard to find—look for the black-and-white photo of the princess near a gunmetal-gray door.) This is the...*

❻ Princess Juliana Daycare

De Wallen is also a residential neighborhood, where ordinary citizens go about their daily lives. Of course, locals need someplace to send their kids. The Princess Juliana Daycare is for newborns to four-year-olds. It was built in the 1970s, when the idea was to mix all dimensions of society together, absorbing the seedy into the decent. I don't know about you, but this location would be a tough sell where I come from.

▶ *Turn left at the canal and continue north along...*

Prostitution in Amsterdam

A customer browses around. A prostitute catches his eye. If the prostitute is interested in his business (prostitutes are selective for their own safety), she winks him over. They talk at the door as she explains her price and what she has to offer. Many are very aggressive at getting the man inside, where the temptation game revs up. A price is agreed on and paid in advance. A typical visit can cost €30-50 for 20 minutes or so. The man goes in. The woman draws the curtain. Where do they actually do it? The rooms look tiny from the street, but these are just display windows. There's a bigger room behind or upstairs that comes with a bed, a sink, and not much else. Or so I've heard.

Are there male prostitutes? Certainly—anything you might want is available somewhere in the Red Light District. But an experiment in the 1990s to put male prostitutes in windows didn't stand up. The district does, however, have plenty of transvestites, who advertise with blue lights rather than red.

❼ Oudezijds Voorburgwal

Pause at the bridge and enjoy the canal and all the old buildings with their charming gables. This area of Amsterdam is one of its most historic and picturesque. But back in the 1970s, this bridge was nicknamed **"Pill Bridge"** for the retail items sold by the seedy guys who used to hang out here. Now it's a pleasant place for a photo-op.

Just past the bridge, at Oudezijds Voorburgwal 40, is one of the city's most worthwhile sights: the **Amstelkring Museum** and Our Lord in the Attic Church. With its triangular gable, this building looks like just another townhouse. But inside, it holds a secret—a small, lavishly decorated place of worship hidden in the attic. Although Amsterdam has long been known

The prostitutes here are self-employed—entrepreneurs, renting space and running their own business. They usually work a four- to eight-hour shift. A good spot costs about €100 for a day shift, and €150 for an evening. Prostitutes are required to keep their premises hygienic, make sure their clients use condoms, and avoid minors.

Popular prostitutes can make about €500 a day. They fill out tax returns, and many belong to a loose union called the Red Thread. The law, not pimps, protects prostitutes. If a prostitute is diagnosed with HIV or AIDS, she loses her license. As shocking as legalized prostitution may seem to some, it's a good example of a pragmatic Dutch solution to a persistent problem.

Although some women may choose prostitution as a lucrative career, others may be forced into it by circumstance—poverty, drug addiction, abusive men, immigration scams, and organized crime syndicates. While the hope is that sex workers are smartly regulated small-businesspeople, in reality the line between victim and entrepreneur is not always so clear.

Amsterdam's current city government is trying to rein in the sex trade and diversify De Wallen. As many as half of the sex businesses here may close over the next few years—not because of prudishness, but to limit the encroachment of organized crime.

for its tolerance, back in the 16th century there was one group they kept in the closet—Catholics. (For more, ✪ see page 118.)

As we stroll up the canal, remember that this neighborhood is Amsterdam's oldest. It sits on formerly marshy land that was reclaimed by diking off the sea's tidal surge. That location gave Amsterdam's merchants easy access to both river trade and the North Sea. Brave Dutch sailors traveled to Africa, America, and Asia, returning with shiploads of exotic goods. The **historical building** (at #14) is from Amsterdam's glory years—around 1580.

With its canals and fine townhouses, Amsterdam became known as the "Venice of the North." The part of the canal we're walking along now is

Pill Bridge, near quaint Little Venice

Pioneering gay bar along Zeedijk street

known as **"Little Venice."** Houses rise directly from the water here, with no quays or streets.

▶ *At the end of the canal, continue straight up a small inclined lane called Sint Olofssteeg. At the top, turn left onto a street called the Zeedijk. Walk along the Zeedijk about 100 yards to the end of the block, where it opens up to a...*

❽ View of the Old Harbor

As you survey the marina, Damrak, and Central Station, imagine the scene in the 1600s. The **old wooden house**—now a café—was once a tavern, sitting right at what was then the water's edge (today's marina was the city's harbor). Boats sailed in and out of the harbor through an opening located where Central Station sits today. (The station was built on reclaimed land.) From there, they could sail along the IJ out to the North Sea.

Amsterdam was home to the Dutch East India Company, the world's first multinational corporation. Goods from all over the world flowed into this harbor, and cargo could be transferred from there to smaller river-trade boats that sailed up the Amstel to Europe's interior. The city grew wealthier and larger, expanding beyond De Wallen to new neighborhoods to the west and south. In its Golden Age, Amsterdam was perhaps the wealthiest city on earth, known as the "warehouse of the world."

Picture a ship tying up in the harbor. The crew has just returned home from a two-year voyage to Bali. They're bringing home fabulous wealth—crates and crates of spices, coffee, and silk. Sailors celebrate their homecoming, spilling onto the Zeedijk. They're greeted by swinging ladies swinging red lanterns. They stop into St. Olaf's chapel to say a prayer of thanks—then head straight to this tavern at Zeedijk 1 and drop anchor for a good Dutch beer. Ahh-hh!

▶ *But our journey continues on. Backtrack along the same street, taking in the sights of Zeedijk street.*

❾ Zeedijk

Pause at the crest of the small bridge. See that green box by the railing? It's part of the city's system of **locks:** Once a day a worker opens up this box and presses a button. The locks open, and the tides flush out the city's canals. Look down—if the gate is open, you might see water flowing in or out. The Zeedijk runs along the top of the "sea dike" that historically protected sea-level Amsterdam from the North Sea tides.

In the early 1600s, Zeedijk street was thriving with overseas trade. But as Amsterdam lost its maritime supremacy to England and France, De Wallen languished. By the 1970s the Zeedijk had become unbelievably sleazy. When I made my first trip here, this street was nicknamed "Heroin Alley." Thousands of addicts wandered like zombies and squatted in old buildings. It was a no-man's-land of junkies fighting amongst themselves, and the police just kept their distance.

But locals took back this historic corner of their city. The first step was legalizing marijuana (considered a relatively harmless drug), followed by a harsh crackdown on hard drugs—heroin, cocaine, and pills. Almost overnight, the illicit drug trade dropped dramatically. Dealers got stiff sentences. Addicts got treatment. Four decades later, the policy seems to have worked, and the Zeedijk belongs to the people of Amsterdam once again.

Continue down the Zeedijk and around the bend. The area has become fairly gentrified, with a mix of ethnic restaurants and bars. The apartment building at #30 (on the right) is new, built in "MIIM" (1998).

The **Café 't Mandje** (at #63) was perhaps Europe's first gay bar, opened in 1927. Today it stands as a memorial to Bet van Beeren, who ran the bar during its heyday in the 1960s. Bet was a lesbian (the original Zee-dyke), and her bar became a safe hangout for gay people. Neckties hang from the ceiling, a reminder of Bet's tradition of scissoring off customers' ties.

▶ *Round the bend on Zeedijk street. Then turn right on narrow Korte Stormsteeg street. This leads quickly back to the canalside red lights. Then go left, before the bridge, along the left side of the canal.*

Social Control

De Wallen has pioneered the Dutch concept of "social control." In Holland, neighborhood security doesn't come from just the police, but from neighbors looking out for each other. If Geert doesn't buy bread for two days, the baker asks around if anyone's seen him. An elderly man feels safe in his home, knowing he's being watched over by the prostitutes next door. Unlike many big cities, there's no chance that anyone here could die or be in trouble and go unnoticed. Video-surveillance cameras keep an eye on the streets. So do prostitutes, who buzz for help if they spot trouble. As you stroll, watch the men who watch the women who watch out for their neighbors—"social control."

⑩ Oudezijds Achterburgwal

We're back in the glitzy Red Light District. This beautiful, tree-lined canal is the heart of this neighborhood's nightlife, playing host to most of the main nightclubs.

The **Banana Bar** (Bananenbar, at #37)—with its erotic Art Nouveau façade—is, basically, a strip club with a-peel: For €50 you get admission for an hour, drinks included. Undressed ladies serve the drinks, perched on the bar. Touching is not allowed, but you can order a banana, and the lady will serve it to you, any way you like. For a full description, step into the lobby.

At Molensteeg, turn right and cross the bridge. The **Erotic Museum** (at #54) is a sex museum that's not as good as the Damrak Sex Museum (see page 120). However, it does uses instructional mannequins to show some of the sex services found in the Red Light District (a prostitute's chambers, an S&M tableau).

Continue south down Oudezijds Achterburgwal. **Theatre Casa Rosso** (lined by pink elephants) is a legit operation. Customers pay a single admission price (no rip-offs or hidden charges) for a strip show. The main event is naked people on stage engaging in sex acts—some simulated, some completely real (€30, www.casarosso.nl).

As you continue south along the canal, you gotta wonder, Why does Amsterdam embrace prostitution and drugs? It's not that the Dutch are any more liberal in their attitudes—they aren't. They're simply more pragmatic.

Scenic canals and sex shows

In the evening, the area is safe and festive.

They've found that when the sex trade goes underground, you get pimps, mobsters, and the spread of STDs. When marijuana is illegal, you get drug dealers, gangs, and violent turf wars. Their solution is to keep these markets legal, and minimize problems through strict regulation.

▶ *Had it with the sleaze? We're almost done. But first...more drugs. Along the right side of the next block, you'll find four cannabis-related establishments.*

⑪ Cannabis Sights

Certain strains of the cannabis plant—particularly mature females of the species *sativa* and *indica*—contain the psychoactive alkaloid tetrahydrocannabinol (THC) that makes you high. The buds, flowers, and leaves (marijuana) can be dried and smoked. The brown sap/resin/pitch that oozes out of the leaves (hashish, a.k.a. hash) can also be dried and smoked. Both produce effects ranging from euphoria to paranoia to the munchies.

The **Cannabis College** (at #124) is a free, nonprofit public study center designed to explain the pros and cons (but mostly pros) of the industrial, medicinal, and recreational uses of the green stuff. You can read about practical hemp products, the medical uses of marijuana, and police prosecution/persecution of cannabis users. Most interesting, you can go downstairs (€3) to see a small cannabis garden, where, as the sign reads, you can "see some real cannabis plants in all their glory."

The **Hemp Gallery** (at #130, admission included in Museum ticket, next) extols the wonders of industrial hemp.

The **Hash, Marijuana, and Hemp Museum** (at #148) is earnestly educational, if you have the patience to read its thorough displays. You'll learn plenty about how valuable the cannabis plant was to Holland during

Several sights teach about marijuana...

...and its notorious history.

the Golden Age. The leafy, green cannabis plant was grown on large plantations. The fibrous stalks (hemp) were made into rope and canvas for ships, and even used to make clothing and lace.

Throughout history, various peoples have used cannabis as a sacred ritual drug—from ancient Scythians and Hindus to modern Nepalis and Afghanis. Modern Rastafarians, following a Bible-based religion centered in Jamaica, smoke cannabis, bob to reggae music, and praise God. All over Amsterdam, you'll see the Rastafarian colors: green, gold, and red, mon.

The museum's highlight is the grow room, where you look through windows at live cannabis plants, some as tall as me. These plants are grown hydroponically (in water, no soil) under grow lights. At a certain stage they're "sexed" to weed out the boring males and "selected" to produce the most powerful strains.

At the museum's exit you'll pass through the **Sensi Seed Bank Store,** which sells weed seeds, how-to books, and knickknacks geared to growers.

Congratulations

We've reached the end of our tour. Dam Square is just two blocks away. (Continue to the end of the block and look right to see the Royal Palace on Dam Square.)

We've seen a lot. We've peeked at locals—from prostitutes to drug pushers to the ghosts of pioneer lesbians to politically active heads with green thumbs. We've talked a bit of history, a little politics, and a lot of sleaze. Congratulations. You've survived. Now, go back to your hotel and take a shower.

Jordaan Walk

This walk is a cultural scavenger hunt. You'll see intimate details of the laid-back Dutch lifestyle that busy tourists don't always appreciate.

The walk takes you from Dam Square—the Times Square of Amsterdam—to the Anne Frank House, and then deep into the characteristic Jordaan neighborhood. Cafés, boutiques, bookstores, and art galleries have gentrified the area. In the Jordaan (yor-DAHN) you'll see things that are commonplace in Amsterdam, but that you won't find in any other city in the world.

Allow about 90 minutes for this short and easygoing walk. It's best by day (before 18:00), when views are nice, and shops and sights are open. (St. Andrew's Hof is closed on Sundays.) You can download this chapter as a free Rick Steves audio tour (✪ see page 167). Bring your camera, as you'll enjoy some of Amsterdam's most charming canal scenes.

THE WALK BEGINS

▶ *Start on Dam Square. Face the Royal Palace, the large building with the green-copper tower. You're facing roughly west, the direction where the Jordaan neighborhood lies. To your right is the New Church (Nieuwe Kerk).*

❶ Dam Square

Dam Square is where the city was born (for more on this square, see page 19). The original residents settled east of here, in the neighborhood now known as the Red Light District. But as Amsterdam grew—from a river-trading village to a worldwide sea-trading empire—the population needed more housing. They started reclaiming land to the west of Dam Square, creating new waterways lined with merchants' townhouses and building a "new" church, the Nieuwe Kerk, to serve these new neighborhoods. This is the area we'll be walking through in the first half of our tour.

By the 1600s—Amsterdam's Golden Age—they needed still more land. They opened up a new development farther west, the Jordaan. It was serviced by the church to the west—the Westerkerk (Western Church), which we'll see. It was also in the 1600s that the Royal Palace was built here on Dam Square. It didn't house royalty, as the name suggests, but was home to the city council. They passed zoning laws and oversaw the rapid expansion of this growing metropolis. Now, let's go see it.

▶ *Facing the Royal Palace, slip to the right, between the palace and the New Church. You'll soon see the facade of the red brick **Magna Plaza Shopping Center.** When it was built in 1899, Magna Plaza was ultra-modern, symbolizing the city's economic revival after two centuries of decline. These days it houses a shopping mall.*

At Magna Plaza, turn right, walking 50 yards down the busy street to the corner of a tiny street called Molsteeg.

❷ Molsteeg

Scan the higgledy-piggledy facades all around you. Are you drunk, high... or just in Amsterdam, where houses settle? Check out the nice line of gables along Molsteeg.

Notice the Mark Raven gallery on the corner. Decades ago, I bought a Mark Raven T-shirt from a street vendor. Now this Amsterdam original, an artist with a distinctive spindly-lined style, has his own upscale shop.

Start on Dam Square, face west, and walk.

Molsteeg is bike-friendly (so watch out!).

Now head down tiny Molsteeg street—but don't walk on the reddish pavement in the middle! That's for bikes. Keep to the sides.

A few steps along, pause at house #5, on the left. Just one window wide, it's typical of the city's old narrow houses. Look up and notice hooks above warehouse doors. This was the typical merchants' design: shop on the ground floor, living space in the middle, and storage in the attic. Houses lean out on purpose, so you can hoist up cargo without bouncing things off the wall. From here this tour's essentially a straight shot west, though the street changes names along the way.

At the intersection with Spuistraat, you'll likely see rows of **bicycles** parked along the street. Amsterdam's 820,000 residents own nearly that many bikes. Bikes outnumber cars here. Many people own two bikes—a long-distance racing bike and a junky in-city bike, often deliberately kept in poor maintenance, so it's less enticing to the many bike thieves in town. Locals are diligent about locking their bikes twice: first the spokes, then a heavy chain attaching the bike to something immovable, such as one of the city's U-shaped hitching racks (called "staples").

The efficient Dutch appreciate a self-propelled machine that travels five times faster than a person on foot, while creating zero pollution, noise, parking problems, or high fuel costs. On a *fiets* (bike), a speedy local can traverse the historic center in about 10 minutes. Biking seems to keep the populace fit and good-looking—people here say that Amsterdam's health clubs are more for networking than for working out. And, when it comes to helmets, few wear them, as many Dutch say "fashion over safety."

▶ *The street opens onto a small space (understandably nicknamed "Big Head Square") that's actually a bridge, straddling the Singel canal. It's called...*

Jordaan Walk

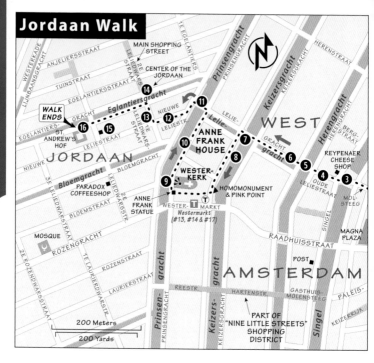

❸ Torensluis Bridge

We haven't quite reached the Jordaan yet, but the atmosphere already seems miles away from busy Dam Square. With cafés, art galleries, and fine benches for picnics, this is a great place to have a seat and take in the Golden Age atmosphere.

Singel Canal: This canal was the original moat running around the old walled city, and this wide bridge was a road to the city gate.

The Houses: Many of these stately townhouses are from the 1600s, when Amsterdam was awash in overseas wealth, the city was expanding, and rich merchants were moving into this new, exclusive neighborhood.

The houses crowd together, shoulder-to-shoulder. They're built on top of thousands of logs hammered vertically into the marshy soil to

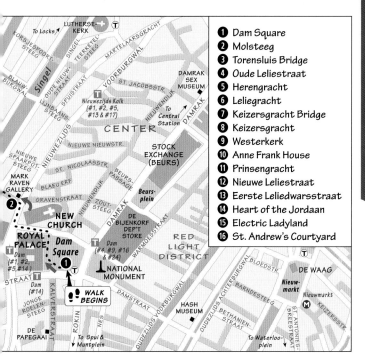

Map legend:
1. Dam Square
2. Molsteeg
3. Torensluis Bridge
4. Oude Leliestraat
5. Herengracht
6. Leliegracht
7. Keizersgracht Bridge
8. Keizersgracht
9. Westerkerk
10. Anne Frank House
11. Prinsengracht
12. Nieuwe Leliestraat
13. Eerste Leliedwarsstraat
14. Heart of the Jordaan
15. Electric Ladyland
16. St. Andrew's Courtyard

provide a foundation. Over the years, they've shifted with the tides, leaving some leaning this way and that. Notice that some of the brick houses have iron rods strapped onto the sides. These act like braces, binding the bricks to an inner skeleton of wood. Almost all Amsterdam houses have big, tall windows to let in as much light as possible.

Although some houses look quite narrow, most of them extend far back, into an *achterhuis* (a back house). As owners were once taxed by the amount of street frontage, it made sense to build up and back.

Multatuli: The "big head" statue honors a writer known by his pen name, Multatuli. Born in Amsterdam in 1820, Multatuli (a.k.a. Eduard Douwes Dekker) did what many young Dutchmen did back then: He sought his fortune in Indonesia, then a colony of the Netherlands. He witnessed

Playful Jordaan residents

Torensluis Bridge—cafés and views

first-hand the hard life of Javanese natives slaving away on Dutch-owned plantations. His semi-autobiographical novel, *Max Havelaar* (1860), raised awareness of Dutch colonial abuses. For his talent and subject matter, Multatuli has been dubbed "the Dutch Rudyard Kipling."

The Locks: In the distance, way down at the north end of Singel, beyond the green dome (a Lutheran church), you can glimpse one of this canal's locks. Those white-flagpole thingies, sprouting at 45-degree angles, are part of the apparatus that opens and shuts the gates. While the canals originated as a way to drain diked-off marshland, they eventually became part of the city's sewer system. They were flushed daily: Just open the locks, and let the North Sea tides come in and out.

The Dutch are credited with inventing locks in the 1300s. (Let's not tell the ancient Chinese.) Besides controlling water flow in the city, they allow ships to pass from higher to lower water levels, and vice versa. It's because of locks that you can ship something by boat from here inland. From this very spot, you could sail a boat upriver, connecting to the Rhine, then the Danube (through a series of locks in Germany), and then sail down the Danube, eventually reaching the Black Sea and Romania.

▶ *Continue west on...*

❹ Oude Leliestraat

On "Old Lily Street," consumers will find plenty of Amsterdam edibles—Reypenaer's cheeses, Puccini's bonbons, Sukabumi's *rijsttafel,* Grey Area's marijuana, Thirsty Dogg's traditional café fare, and *shoarmas*—everything but lilies. The Reypenaer cheese shop gives out free tasty samples, and has a classroom in the basement for daily in-depth

Gables

Along the rooftops, Amsterdam's famous gables are false fronts to enhance roofs that are, generally, sharply pitched. Gables come in all shapes and sizes. They might be ornamented with animal and human heads, garlands, urns, scrolls, and curlicues. Despite their infinite variety, most belong to a few distinct types. See how many of these you can spot.

A simple "point" gable just follows the triangular shape of a normal pitched roof. A "bell" gable is shaped like...well, guess. "Step" gables are triangular in shape and lined with steps; these are especially popular in Belgium. The one with a rectangular protrusion at the peak is called a "spout" gable. "Neck" gables rise up vertically from a pair of sloping "shoulders." "Cornice" gables make pointed roofs look classically horizontal. (There's probably even a "clark" gable, but frankly, I don't give a damn.)

Point   Bell   Step

Spout   Neck   Cornice

See no reefer, hear no reefer at Grey Area.   Herengracht—a canal of gabled townhouses

cheese-tasting sessions (for a fee, reserve at 020/320-6333, www.wijngaard kaas.nl).

The Grey Area's green-and-white decal in the window identifies it as #092 in the city's licensing program for marijuana-dealing "coffeeshops." While smoking marijuana is essentially legal here, the café's name refers to the murky back-side of the marijuana business—how coffeeshops get their supply from wholesalers. That's the "gray area" that Dutch laws have yet to sort out. This esteemed coffeeshop, which works with the best boutique growers in Holland, regularly wins big at Amsterdam's annual Cannabis Cup Awards—a "high" honor, to be sure.

▶ *The next canal is the...*

❺ Herengracht

During the Dutch Golden Age boom in the 1600s, Amsterdam expanded, adding this canal. It's named for the *heren,* the wealthy city merchants who lined it with their mansions. Even today, this is a high-rent district. (Notice that zoning here forbids houseboats.)

Check out the house that's kitty-corner across the bridge, at Herengracht 150. It has features you'll find on many old Amsterdam buildings. On the roof, rods support the false-front gable. Also, notice how long the building is. Most Amsterdam buildings, like this one, are much bigger than they appear from the front.

Find the parking sign along Herengracht (on the left) instructing motorists to put money in the meter at the end of the block. Parking is a major problem in a city like this, designed for boats, not cars.

▶ *Continue west, walking along...*

❻ Leliegracht

This is one of the city's prettiest small canals, lined with trees and crossed by a series of arched bridges. There are some 400 such bridges in Amsterdam. It's a pleasant street of trendy furniture shops and bookstores.

Notice that some buildings have staircases leading down below the street level to residences. Looking up, you'll see the characteristic beams jutting out from the top with a cargo-hoisting hook on the end. Attach a pulley to that, and you can lift up a sofa and send it through a big upper-story window—much easier than lugging it up a long, narrow staircase.

▶ *Continue on to the next canal and pause on the* ❼ ***Keizersgracht Bridge*** *to take in the view. There's a nice row of gables, and the colorful crown of the Westerkerk church tower rises above the rooftops.*

After the bridge, we'll take a detour off our westward route, and veer left along the Keizersgracht canal, making our way to the Westerkerk.

❽ Keizersgracht

Walk south about 100 yards along the canal, with an eye toward the church tower.

Homomonument: You'll reach a set of steps leading down to the water, where a triangular pink stone juts into the canal. This is part of the so-called Homomonument, Amsterdam's AIDS memorial. If you survey the square, you'll see that the pink triangle is just one of three triangles between here and the church. These are contained in a single large triangle that comprises the Homomonument. The pink-triangle design reclaims the symbol that the Nazis used in concentration camps to label homosexual men. It's also a reminder of the persecution gay people still experience today. You may see flowers or cards left here by friends and loved ones. Nearby is a souvenir kiosk called Pink Point, with information on gay and lesbian Amsterdam.

The green metal structure near the Homomonument is a public urinal. It offers just enough privacy. City trucks circulate around town on a regular basis, suds-ing them down.

Westermarkt Square: In the square between the church and busy Raadhuisstraat, you'll find two very Dutch kiosks. One sells french fries; when it's closed, the shutters feature funny paintings putting *friet*s into great masterpieces of Western art. The other sells fresh herring. Try one. You get a fresh herring with pickles and onion on a paper plate and instructions from the friendly merchant on how to eat it.

A memorial to AIDS victims   The crown of the Westerkerk

The sweet little **statue** is of Anne Frank, who holed up with her family in a house just down the block from here. Anne was born in Germany, but her family moved to Holland when the Nazis took power in their native land. But in 1940, Germany invaded the Netherlands; they entered Amsterdam by marching down (nearby) Radhuisstraat. The Frank family went underground. More on that tragic story in just a bit.

▶ *For now, turn your attention to the impressive...*

⑨ Westerkerk

Look up at the towering spire. The crown shape was a gift of the Habsburg emperor, Maximilian I. As a thanks for a big loan, the city got permission to use the Habsburg royal symbol. The tower also displays the symbol of Amsterdam, with its three Xs.

The Westerkerk (Western Church) was built in 1631, as the city was expanding out from Dam Square. Rembrandt's buried inside...but no one knows where. You can pop into the church for free, or pay to climb to the tower balcony (just below the *XXX*) for a grand view (church generally open April-Sept Mon-Sat 11:00-15:00; for tower-climb details, ✪ see page 120).

The church tower has a carillon that chimes every 15 minutes. At other times, it plays full songs. Invented by Dutch bellmakers in the 1400s, a carillon is a set of bells of different sizes and pitches. There's a live musician inside the tower who plays a keyboard to make the music. Mozart, Vivaldi, and Bach—all of whom lived during the heyday of the carillon—wrote music that sounds great on this unique instrument. During World War II, the Westerkerk's carillon played every day. This hopeful sound reminded Anne Frank that there was, indeed, an outside world.

> *Continue past the church, walking north along the canal, past the long line of tourists marking the entrance to the ever-popular...*

⑩ Anne Frank House

Though we won't go inside on this walking tour, it's worth pausing here at Prinsengracht #267. This was the office of Anne Frank's father, Otto, who ran a spice business. It was here that eight Amsterdam Jews hid from Nazi persecution, including 13-year-old Anne Frank. The family's hiding

A statue to Anne Frank remembers those who hid from the Nazis in the back of a nearby house.

place was way in the back part of the building—making this the world's best-known *actherhuis* (back house). (✪ See the Anne Frank House Tour chapter.)

▶ *Continue to the next bridge and turn left. Stop at its summit, mid-canal, for a view of...*

⓫ Prinsengracht

The "Princes' Canal" runs through one of the most livable areas in town. It's lined with houseboats, some of the city's estimated 2,500. These small vessels were once cargo ships—but by the 1930s, they had become obsolete, replaced by more modern craft. They found a new use, as houseboats lining the canals of Amsterdam, where dry land was so limited and pricey.

Today, their former cargo holds are fashioned into elegant, cozy living rooms. The once-powerful engines have generally been removed to make room for more living space. Moorage spots are prized and grandfathered in, making some of the junky old boats worth more than you'd think. Houseboaters can plug hoses and cables into outlets along the canals to get water and electricity.

Notice the canal traffic. The official speed limit on canals is about four miles per hour. At night, boats must have running lights on the top, the side, and the stern. Most boats are small and low, designed to glide under the city's bridges. The Prinsengracht bridge is average height, with less than seven feet of headroom (it varies with the water level); some bridges have less than six feet. Boaters need good maps to tell them the height, which is crucial for navigating. Police boats roam on the lookout for anyone CUI (cruising under the influence).

▶ *The recommended Café 't Smalle—though not visible from here—is nearby (✪ see page 150). Once you cross Prinsengracht, you enter what's officially considered the Jordaan neighborhood. Facing west (toward Café de Prins), cross the bridge and veer left down...*

⓬ Nieuwe Leliestraat

Welcome to the quiet Jordaan. Built in the 1600s as a working-class housing area, it's now home to artists and yuppies. The name Jordaan probably was not derived from the French *jardin*—but given the neighborhood's garden-like ambience, it seems like it should have been.

Have your ultra-sharp "traveler's eyes" trained on all the tiny details of

Amsterdam life. Notice house #2. While parking is generally not allowed in this area, this prime space—complete with a plug-in—reserves a spot for those investing in an electric car. Signs warn speeding drivers of the speed bumps: *Let op!* and watch out for *drempels*.

Notice how the pragmatic Dutch deal with junk mail. On the doors, stickers next to mail slots say *Nee* or *Ja* (no or yes), telling the postman if they'll accept or refuse junk mail. Residents are allowed a "front-yard garden" as long as it's no more than one sidewalk tile wide. The red metal bollards known as *Amsterdammertjes* ("little Amsterdammers") have been bashing balls since the 1970s, when they were put in to stop people from parking on the sidewalks. Though many apartments have windows right on the street, the neighbors don't stare and the residents don't care.

▶ *At the first intersection, turn right onto...*

⑬ Eerste Leliedwarsstraat

Pause on this tiny lane. Imagine the frustrations of home ownership here. The ugly modern buildings you see date from the 1960s and '70s. This was before the gentrification of the 1980s, when the city started writing more restrictive building codes.

Check out house #9. Here, a run-down historic home was torn down, replaced by a building with modern heating and plumbing. Now move ahead to #5. Its owners missed the window of time when a cheap rebuild was allowed, and now they can't get permission. Across the street, #2A obviously had the cash to do a first-class sprucing up. Even newly renovated homes must preserve their funky leaning angles and original wooden beams. They're certainly nice to look at, but absolutely maddening if you own an old building and aren't rich.

Some residents live on houseboats.

Want junk mail? Tell the postman yes or no.

▶ *Just ahead, walk out to the middle of the bridge over the next canal (Egelantiersgracht). This is what I think of as...*

⑭ The Heart of the Jordaan

For me, this bridge and its surroundings capture the essence of the Jordaan. Take it all in: the bookstores, art galleries, working artists' studios, and small cafés full of rickety tables. Look down the quiet canal. It's lined with trees and old, narrow buildings with gables—classic Amsterdam.

Look north, farther down the street beyond the bridge. This lane, called Tweede Egelantiers Dwarsstraat, is the laid-back Jordaan neighborhood's main shopping-and-people street. If you venture down there, you'll find boutiques, galleries, antique stores, hair salons, restaurants, and cafés.

Now turn around and look south at the Westerkerk, and you'll see a completely different view of the church than most tourists get. Framed by narrow streets, crossed with streetlamp wires, and looming over shoppers on bicycles—to me, this is the church in its best light.

Backtrack to the base of the bridge, then turn right. Walk west along Egelantiersgracht.

⑮ Electric Ladyland and other Sights

As you walk along Egelantiersgracht, check out the **boats.** Junky old boats litter the canal. Some aren't worth maintaining and are left abandoned. As these dinghies fill with rainwater and start to rot, the city confiscates them and stores them in a big lot. Unclaimed boats are auctioned off three times a year. But most boats are well used, and even the funkiest scows can become cruising Love Boats when the sun goes down.

Jordaan's greatest sight: everyday life

Nick welcomes you to his blacklight museum.

St. Andrew's Courtyard—low-key doorway into this quiet slice of the Jordaan

Electric Ladyland: At the first intersection, turn left onto Tweede Leliedwarsstraat, and walk a few steps to #5. This small shop, with a flowery window display, calls itself "The First Museum of Fluorescent Art." Its funky facade hides an illuminated wonderland within—a tiny exhibit of black-light art. Nick Padalino—one cool cat who really found his niche in life—enjoys personally demonstrating the fluorescence found in unexpected places, from minerals to stamps to candy to the tattoo on his arm. Wow. (€5, Tue-Sat 13:00-18:00, closed Sun-Mon).

About 100 yards farther down the street is the **Paradox Coffeeshop,** a friendly, mellow place for the nervous American who wants to go local (see page 173).

▶ *To reach our last stop, backtrack to the canal and turn left, then walk a few dozen yards to Egelantiersgracht #107, the entrance to...*

⑯ St. Andrew's Courtyard (Sint-Andrieshof)

The black door is marked *Sint-Andrieshof 107 t/m 145.* The doorway looks private, but it's the public entrance to a set of residences. It's generally open during daytime hours, except on Sundays. Enter quietly; you may have to push hard on the door. Go inside and continue on into a tiny garden courtyard surrounded by a dozen or so residences. Take a seat on a bench. This is one of the city's scores of similar courtyards, called *hofjes*—subsidized residences built around a courtyard, and funded by churches, charities, and the city for low-income widows and pensioners.

And this is where our tour ends—in a tranquil world that seems right out of a painting by Vermeer. You're just blocks from the bustle of Amsterdam, but it feels like another world. You're immersed in the Jordaan, where everything's in its place, and life seems very good.

Anne Frank House Tour

On May 10, 1940, Germany's Luftwaffe began bombing Schiphol Airport, preparing to invade the Netherlands. The Dutch army fought back, and the Nazis responded by leveling Rotterdam. Within a week, the Netherlands surrendered, Queen Wilhelmina fled to Britain, and Nazi soldiers goose-stepped past the Westerkerk and into Dam Square, where they draped huge swastikas on the Royal Palace. A five-year occupation began.

The Anne Frank House immerses you, in a very immediate way, in the struggles and pains of the war years. Walk through rooms where, for two years, eight Amsterdam Jews hid from Nazi persecution. Though they were eventually discovered, and seven of the eight died in concentration camps, their story has an uplifting twist—the diary of Anne Frank, an affirmation of the human spirit that cannot be crushed.

ORIENTATION

Cost: €9, covered by Museumkaart but not I amsterdam Card.

Hours: March 15-Sept 14 daily 9:00-21:00, Sat and July-Aug until 22:00; Sept 15-March 14 daily 9:00-19:00, Sat until 21:00; last entry 30 minutes before closing. Closed for Yom Kippur.

Avoiding Lines: Skip the long ticket-buying line (which is especially bad in the daytime during summer) by purchasing your ticket and reserving an entry time online at annefrank.org (€0.50/person fee). Museumkaart holders can purchase an online reservation without buying a separate Anne Frank House ticket. Book as soon as you're sure of your itinerary.

With your ticket in hand, you can skip the line and ring the buzzer at the low-profile door marked *Entrance: Reservations Only*. Without a reservation, try arriving when the museum opens (at 9:00) or after 18:00.

Getting There: It's at Prinsengracht 267, near Westerkerk and about a 20-minute walk from Central Station. You can also take tram #13, #14, or #17—or bus #170 or #172—to the Westermarkt stop, about a block south of the museum's entrance.

Information: The museum has excellent information in English throughout. Use this chapter as background, and then let the displays and videos tell you more. Tel. 020/556-7100, annefrank.org. Note that the house has many steep, narrow stairways.

Length of This Tour: Allow one hour.

Baggage Check: Big bags are not allowed (daypacks are OK), and there's no place to check them.

Eating: The museum café serves simple fare and has good views (daily 9:30-18:00). For more suggestions, ✪ see page 150.

THE TOUR BEGINS

We'll walk through the rooms where Anne Frank's family and four other Jews hid for 25 months. The front half of the building, facing the canal, remained the offices and warehouses of an operating business. The back half, where the Franks and others lived, was the Secret Annex, its entrance concealed by a bookcase.

▶ *After the ticket desk, enter the ground-floor exhibit. After viewing the important five-minute video, go upstairs to the offices/storerooms of the front half of the building.*

First Floor: Offices

From these offices, Otto Frank ran a successful business called Opekta, selling spices and pectin for making jelly. When the Nazis gained

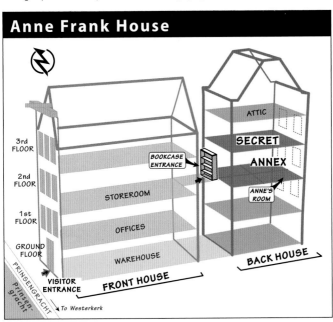

Anne Frank House

ATTIC

3rd FLOOR

SECRET

ANNEX

2nd FLOOR

BOOKCASE ENTRANCE

STOREROOM

ANNE'S ROOM

1st FLOOR

OFFICES

GROUND FLOOR

WAREHOUSE

BACK HOUSE

PRINSENGRACHT / Prinsen-gracht

VISITOR ENTRANCE

FRONT HOUSE

↓ To Westerkerk

Otto Frank—Anne's father

Miep and Jan Gies helped the Franks hide.

power in Germany in 1933, Otto moved his family from Frankfurt to tolerant Amsterdam, hoping for a better life.

Photos and displays show Otto with some of his colleagues. During the Nazi occupation, while the Frank family hid in the back of the building, these brave people kept Otto's business running, secretly bringing supplies to the Franks. Miep Gies, Otto's secretary (see her in the video), brought food every few days, while bookkeeper Victor Kugler cheered up Anne with the latest movie magazines.

▶ Go upstairs to the...

Second Floor: Storeroom

Two models show the two floors where Anne, her family, and four others lived. Dollhouse furniture helps you envision life in the now-bare living quarters. All told, eight people lived in a tiny apartment smaller than 1,000 square feet.

At first the Nazi overlords were lenient toward, even friendly with, the vanquished Dutch. But soon they began imposing restrictions that affected one in ten Amsterdammers—that is, Jews. Jews had to wear yellow-star patches and register with the police. They were banned from movie theaters and trams, and even forbidden to ride bikes.

In February of 1941, the Nazis started rounding up Amsterdam's Jews, shipping them by train to "work camps," which, in reality, were transit stations on the way to death camps in the east. Outraged, the people of Amsterdam called a general strike that shut down the city for two days... but the Nazis responded with even harsher laws.

In July of 1942, Anne's sister Margot got her **call-up notice** for a "work-force project." Otto handed over the keys to the business to his

"Aryan" colleagues, sent a final postcard to relatives, gave the family cat to a neighbor, spread rumors that they were fleeing to Switzerland, and prepared his family to "dive under" (*onderduik,* as it was called) into hiding.

Photos of the people in hiding put faces on the eight people—all Jewish—who eventually inhabited the Secret Annex. First was the Frank family—Otto and Edith and their daughters, 13-year-old Anne and 16-year-old Margot. A week later, they were joined by the Van Pels (called the "Van Daans" in her diary), with their teenage son, Peter. A few months later, Fritz Pfeffer (called "Mr. Dussel" in the diary) was invited in.

▶ *It's now time to enter the hiding place. At the back of the second floor storeroom is the clever hidden passageway into the Secret Annex.*

SECRET ANNEX

The Bookcase Entrance

On a rainy Monday morning, July 6, 1942, the Frank family—wearing extra clothes to avoid carrying suspicious suitcases—breathed their last fresh air, took a long look at the Prinsengracht canal, and disappeared into the

This bookcase swung open to reveal a hidden passageway into the Secret Annex.

back part of the building, where they spent the next two years. Victor Kugler concealed the entrance to the annex with this swinging bookcase, stacked with business files.

Though not exactly a secret (since it's hard to hide an entire building), the annex was a typical back house *(achterhuis)*, a common feature in Amsterdam buildings, and the Nazis had no reason to suspect anything on the premises of the legitimate Opekta business.

▶ *Pass through the bookcase entrance into...*

Otto, Edith, and Margot's Room

The family carried on life as usual. Otto read Dickens' **Sketches by Boz,** Edith read from a **prayer book** in their native German, and the children continued their studies, with Margot taking **Latin lessons** by correspondence course. They avidly followed the course of the war by radio broadcasts and news from their helpers. As the tides of war slowly turned and it appeared they might one day be saved from the Nazis, Otto tracked the Allied advance on a **map** of Normandy.

The room is very small, even without the furniture. Imagine yourself and two fellow tourists confined here for two years...

Pencil lines on the wall track Margot's and Anne's heights, marking the point at which these growing lives were cut short.

Anne Frank's Room

Pan the room clockwise to see some of the young girl's idols in photos and clippings she pasted there herself: American actor Robert Stack, the future Queen Elizabeth II as a child, matinee idol Rudy Vallee, figure-skating actress Sonja Henie, and, on the other wall, actress Greta Garbo, actor Ray Milland, Renaissance man Leonardo da Vinci, and actress Ginger Rogers.

Out the window (which had to be blacked out) is the back courtyard, which had a chestnut tree and a few buildings. (In 2010, the tree, which Anne had greatly enjoyed, toppled in a storm.) These things, along with the Westerkerk bell chiming every 15 minutes, represented the borders of Anne's "outside world." Imagine Anne sitting here at a small desk, writing in her diary.

In November of 1942, the Franks invited a Jewish neighbor to join them, and Anne was forced to share the tiny room. Fritz Pfeffer (known in the diary as "Mr. Dussel") was a middle-aged dentist with whom Anne didn't get along.

Life in the Annex

By day, it's enforced silence, so no one can hear them in the offices. They whisper, tiptoe, and step around squeaky places in the floor. The windows are blacked out, so they can't even look outside. They read or study, and Anne writes in her diary.

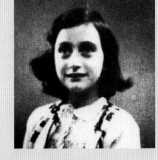

At night and on weekends, when the offices close, one or two might sneak downstairs to listen to Winston Churchill's BBC broadcasts on the office radio. Everyone's spirits rise and sink with news of Allied victories and setbacks.

Anne's diaries make clear the tensions, petty quarrels, and domestic politics of eight people living under intense pressure. Mr. Van Pels annoys Anne, but he gets along well with Margot. Anne never gets used to Mr. Pfeffer, who is literally invading her space. Most troublesome of all, pubescent Anne often strikes sparks with her mom. (Anne's angriest comments about her mother were deleted from early editions of the published diary.)

Despite their hardships, the group feels guilty: They have shelter, while so many other Jews are being rounded up and sent off.

As the war progresses, they endure long nights when the house shakes from Allied air raids, and Anne cuddles up in her dad's bed.

Boredom tinged with fear—this existentialist hell is captured so well in Anne's journal.

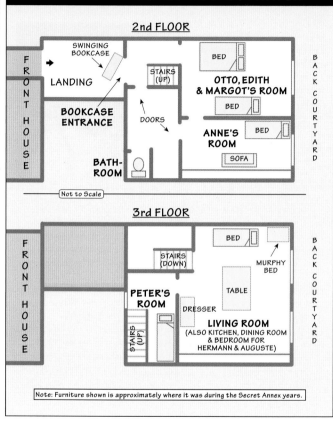

Anne Frank House: Secret Annex

2nd FLOOR

FRONT HOUSE

LANDING

SWINGING BOOKCASE

BOOKCASE ENTRANCE

STAIRS (UP)

DOORS

BED

OTTO, EDITH & MARGOT'S ROOM

BED

ANNE'S ROOM

BED

SOFA

BATH-ROOM

BACK COURTYARD

Not to Scale

3rd FLOOR

FRONT HOUSE

STAIRS (DOWN)

PETER'S ROOM

STAIRS (UP)

DRESSER

BED

MURPHY BED

TABLE

LIVING ROOM
(ALSO KITCHEN, DINING ROOM & BEDROOM FOR HERMANN & AUGUSTE)

BACK COURTYARD

Note: Furniture shown is approximately where it was during the Secret Annex years.

The Bathroom

The eight inhabitants shared this bathroom. During the day, they didn't dare flush the toilet.

▶ *Ascend the steep staircase—silently—to the...*

Common Living Room

This was also the kitchen and dining room. Otto Frank was well off, and early on, the annex was well-stocked with food. Miep Gies would dutifully take their shopping list, buy food for her "family" of eight, and secretly lug it up to them. Buying such large quantities in a coupon-rationed economy was highly suspect, but she knew a sympathetic grocer (a block away on Leliegracht) who was part of a ring of Amsterdammers risking their lives to help the Jews.

The **menu** for a special dinner lists soup, roast beef, salad, potatoes, rice, dessert, and coffee. Later, as war and German restrictions plunged Holland into poverty and famine, they survived on canned foods and dried kidney beans.

At night, the living room became sleeping quarters for Hermann and Auguste van Pels.

Peter van Pels' Room

On Peter's 16th birthday, he got a Monopoly-like board game called "The Broker" as a present.

Initially, Anne was cool toward Peter, but after two years together, a courtship developed, and their flirtation culminated in a kiss.

The staircase (no visitor access) leads up to where they stored their food. Anne loved to steal away here for a bit of privacy. At night they'd open a hatch to let in fresh air.

One hot August day, Otto was in this room helping Peter learn English, when they looked up to see a man with a gun. The hiding was over.

▶ *From here we leave the Secret Annex, returning to the Opekta store-room and offices in the front house. As you work your way downstairs, you'll see a number of exhibits on the aftermath of this story.*

THE AFTERMATH

Front House: The Arrest, Deportation, and Auschwitz Exhibits

They went quietly. On August 4, 1944, a German policeman accompanied by three Dutch Nazis pulled up in a car, politely entered the Opekta office, and went straight to the bookcase entrance. No one knows who tipped them off. The police gave the surprised hiders time to pack. They demanded their valuables and stuffed them into Anne's briefcase...after dumping her diaries onto the floor.

Taken in a van to Gestapo headquarters, the eight were processed in an efficient, bureaucratic manner, then placed on a train to Westerbork, a concentration camp northeast of the city (see their 3-inch-by-5-inch **registration cards**).

From there they were locked in a car on a normal passenger train and sent to Auschwitz, a Nazi extermination camp in Poland (see the **transport list,** which includes "Anneliese Frank"). On the platform at Auschwitz, they were "forcibly separated from each other" (as Otto later reported) and sent to different camps. Anne and Margot were sent to Bergen-Belsen.

Don't miss the **video** of one of Anne's former neighbors who, by chance, ended up at Bergen-Belsen with Anne. In English she describes their reunion as they talked through a barbed-wire fence shortly before Anne died. She says of Anne, "She didn't have any more tears."

Anne and Margot both died of typhus in March of 1945, only weeks before the camp was liberated. Five of the other original eight were either gassed or died of disease. Only Otto survived.

The Franks' story was that of Holland's Jews. The seven who died were among the more than 100,000 Dutch Jews killed during the war years. (Before the war, 135,000 Jews lived in the Netherlands.) Of Anne's school class of 87 Jews, only 20 survived.

▶ *The next room is devoted to Anne's father.*

The Otto Frank Room

Listen to a 1967 video of Anne's father talking about how the diaries were discovered in the annex. The case holds a rotating display: You may find notebooks that Otto kept during the hiding period, or letters he wrote after the war as he tried to get Anne's diaries published.

Often on display (either here or elsewhere) are video interviews with survivors. Miep Gies—who passed away in 2010 at the age of 100—describes how she found Anne's diaries in the Secret Annex following the arrest, and gave them to Otto after the war. Another video shows Otto's reaction. Though the annex's furniture was ransacked during the arrest, the rooms remained virtually untouched, and we see them today much as they were.

▶ Downstairs you come to...

The Diaries

See Anne's three diaries, which were published after the war. Anne received the first diary (with a red-plaid binding) as a birthday present when she turned 13, shortly before the family went into hiding. She wrote her diary in the form of a letter to an imaginary friend named Kitty. The other two diaries were written in school-exercise books. Also on display are a book of Anne's short stories, a notebook she kept of favorite quotes, and some loose-leaf pages on which she rewrote and revised parts of her diary.

Otto decided to have the diaries published, and in 1947, *De Achterhuis (The Back House)* appeared in Dutch, soon followed by many translations,

Anne's diaries chronicled both her tedious life in hiding and her expansive dreams.

a play, and a movie. While she was alive, Anne herself had recognized the uniqueness of her situation and had been in the process of revising her diaries, preparing them to one day be published.

▶ Continue downstairs to the ground-floor exhibits.

The Moral

You'll learn of Otto's struggles to save the house from demolition and turn it into a museum.

An interactive exhibit called "Free2Choose" presents various moral dilemmas, in which well-meaning people struggle to do the right thing. You can vote your own opinion. The point? To keep visitors from leaving the museum with pat feelings of easy moral clarity.

The Anne Frank Foundation is obviously concerned that we learn from Europe's Nazi nightmare. The thinking that made the Holocaust possible still survives. Even today, some groups promote the notion that the Holocaust never occurred and contend that stories like Anne Frank's are only a hoax. It was Otto Frank's dream that visitors come away from the Anne Frank House with an indelible impression—and a better ability to apply these lessons to our contemporary challenges.

Anne's much-read diary has helped turn the Franks' personal struggle into a universal story.

Sights in Amsterdam

One of Amsterdam's delights is that it has perhaps more specialty museums than any other city its size. From houseboats to sex, from marijuana to Old Masters, you can find a museum to suit your interests.

The following sights are arranged by neighborhood for handy sightseeing. When you see a ✪ in a listing, it means the sight is covered in much more depth in one of my walks or self-guided tours.

A few quick tips: Avoid long ticket lines at the Anne Frank House, Van Gogh Museum, and Rijksmuseum by getting tickets in advance (✪ see page 167). A sightseeing pass (the Museumkaart or I amsterdam Card) can save time and money (✪ see page 168). Most sights have plenty of English explanations. For canal boat tours, ✪ see page 174. Finally, remember that though the city has several must-see museums, its best attraction is its own carefree ambience.

Amsterdam Sights

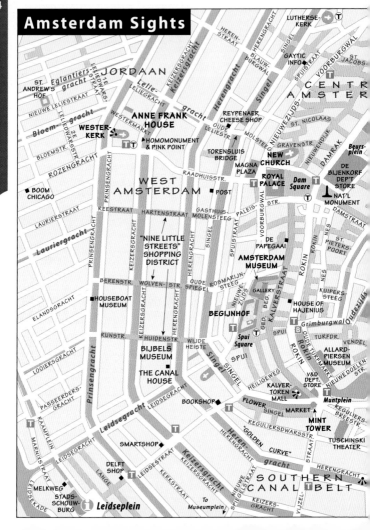

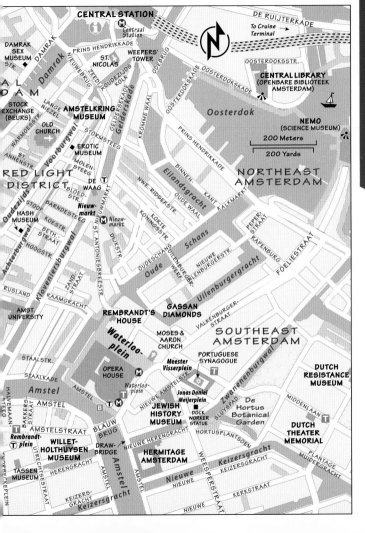

CENTRAL STATION
DE RUIJTERKADE
To Cruise Terminal

PRINS HENDRIKKADE
Centraal Station
OOSTERDOKSSTR.

DAMRAK SEX MUSEUM STR.
Damrak
NIEUWEBRUG
ST. NICOLAS
WEEPERS' TOWER
ODEBRUG
OOSTERDOKSKADE

AL DAM
ZEEDIJK
OUDEZIJDS KOLK
OOSTERDOKSKADE
CENTRAL LIBRARY
(OPENBARE BIBLIOTEEK AMSTERDAM)

STOCK EXCHANGE (BEURS)
LANGE NIEZEL
AMSTELKRING MUSEUM
GELDERSEKADE
KROMME WAAL
Oosterdok
NEMO (SCIENCE MUSEUM)

OLD CHURCH
Voorburgwal
STORMSTEEG
PRINS HENDRIKKADE
200 Meters

ST. ANNENSTR.
EROTIC MUSEUM
MOLEN-STEEG
200 Yards

RED LIGHT DISTRICT
DE WAAG
BLOED-STR.
BINNEN
Eilandsgracht
KANT
KALKMARKT
NORTHEAST AMSTERDAM

Oudezijds
HASH MUSEUM
BARNDESTEEG
Nieuw-markt
NWE RIDDERSTR.
OUDE WAAL

Achterburgwal
STOOF
KOESTR.
ST. ANTONIESBREESTR.
Nieuw-markt
KORTE KONINGSSTR.
PEPER-STRAAT

BETH-STRAAT
HOOGSTR.
DIJKSTR.
Schans
NIEUWE MOLENBURGERSTR.
RAPENBURG

RUSLAND
KLOVENIERSBURGWAL
ZAND-STRAAT
OUDESCHANS
UILENBURGER-WERF
Oude
NIEUWE UILENBURGERSTR.
FOELIESTRAAT

AMST. UNIVERSITY
RAAMGRACHT
Uilenburgergracht

RembrandT'S HOUSE
GASSAN DIAMONDS
VALKENBURGER-STRAAT
SOUTHEAST AMSTERDAM

Waterloo-plein
MOSES & AARON CHURCH
VALKENBURGER-STRAAT

STAALSTR.
OPERA HOUSE
Meester Visserplein
PORTUGUESE SYNAGOGUE
Zwanenburgwal
DUTCH RESISTANCE MUSEUM

STAALKADE
Waterloo-plein
NIEUWE AMSTELSTR.
Jonas Daniel Meijerplein
SLUYSPAD
MIDDENLAAN

Amstel
AMSTEL
JEWISH HISTORY MUSEUM
DOCK WORKER STATUE
De Hortus Botanical Garden

HAVEMAN STEEG
BAKKERS-STRAAT
AMSTEL
AMSTELSTRAAT
BLAUW BRUG
NIEUWE HERENGRACHT
HORTUSPLANTSOEN
DUTCH THEATER MEMORIAL

Rembrandt-plein
WILLET-HOLTHUYSEN MUSEUM
DRAW-BRIDGE
NIEUWE HERENGRACHT
PLANTAGE MUIDERGRACHT

TASSEN MUSEUM
UTRECHTSESTRAAT
AMSTELSTRAAT
HERENGRACHT
HERMITAGE AMSTERDAM
Keizersgracht
KEIZERSGRACHT

KEIZERS-GRACHT
KEIZERS-GRACHT
Keizersgracht
NIEUWE
NIEUWE WEESPERSTRAAT
KERKSTRAAT
NIEUWE

Central Amsterdam

The historic center extends from Central Station to the Mint Tower—the area enclosed by the Singel canal. The following sights are all either on or within a 10-minute walk of Dam Square.

▲Royal Palace (Koninklijk Huis)

Built as a lavish City Hall (1648-1655)—when Amsterdam was the richest city on the planet, awash in profit from trade—this building was renamed the "Royal Palace" when Louis Bonaparte was made king of Holland. The Dutch royal family (the House of Orange) lived here, and current King Willem-Alexander numbers it among his official residences. About 20 of the palace's lavishly decorated rooms are open to the public.

The highlight is the huge, white Citizens' Hall—120 feet by 60 feet by 90 feet, and lit by eight big chandeliers. At the far end, a statue of Atlas holds the globe of the world, and the ceiling painting shows Amsterdam triumphant amid the clouds of heaven. On the floor, inlaid maps show the known world circa 1750 (back when the West Coast of the US still had unmapped territory). The hall is used today for hosting foreign dignitaries and for royal family wedding receptions.

You'll see the room where Louis Bonaparte's throne once sat (in front of the fireplace), a room of impressive Empire Style furniture (high-polished wood with Neoclassical motifs), and the bedroom of former Queen Beatrix. The palace's rich chandeliers, paintings, statues, and furniture reflect Amsterdam's historic status as the center of global trade.

▶ *€7.50, includes audioguide, open daily 11:00-17:00 but often closed for official business, tel. 020/620-4060, paleisamsterdam.nl.*

New Church (Nieuwe Kerk)

Barely newer than the "Old" Church (located in the Red Light District), this 15th-century sanctuary has a spare interior, lots of tradition (royal weddings and coronations), and popular temporary exhibits.

✪ See page 24 of the Amsterdam City Walk chapter.

▲Begijnhof

Stepping into this tiny, idyllic courtyard in the city center, you escape into the charm of old Amsterdam.

✪ See page 27 of the Amsterdam City Walk chapter.

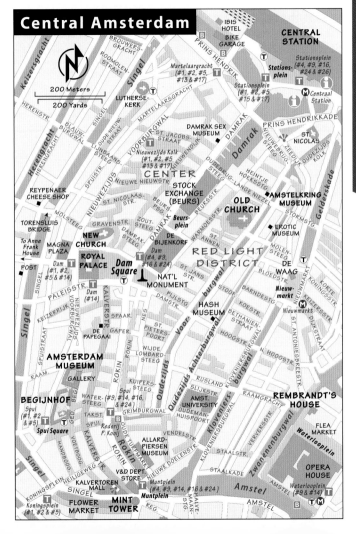

Central Amsterdam

200 Meters
200 Yards

IBIS HOTEL
BIKE GARAGE
CENTRAL STATION

BROUWERS-GRACHT
ROOMOLEN-STRAAT
PRINS HENDRIK
Stationsplein (#4, #9, #16, #24 & #26)
Stations-plein
Centraal Station
Stationsplein (#1, #2, #5 #15 & #17)

Keizersgracht
Singel
HERENSTR.
LUTHERSE-KERK

Martelaargracht (#1, #2, #5, #13 & #17)

PRINS HENDRIKKADE

Herengracht
BLAUW-BURGWAL
OUDE NIEUW-DIJK
St. JACOBS-STRAAT
VOORBURGWAL
DAMRAK SEX MUSEUM
DAMRAK
ST. NICOLAS
ZEEDIJK
OUDEZIJDS KOLK

Herengracht
LIJNBANS-STEEG
Nieuwezijds Kolk (#1, #2, #5 #13 & #17)
NIEUWENDIJK
CENTER
NIEUWE NIEUWZ.STR.
STOCK EXCHANGE (BEURS)
OUDEBRUG-STEEG
HEINTJE HOEKSTEEG
LANGE NIEZEL

REYPENAER CHEESE SHOP
SPUISTR.
ST. NICOLAAS-STR.
GRAVENSTR.
Beurs-plein
WARMOESSTR.
OLD CHURCH
AMSTELKRING MUSEUM
Geldersekade
STORMSTR.

TORENSLUIS BRIDGE
MOLSTEEG
ZOUT-STEEG
DAMRAK-STEEG
DE BIJENKORF
ST. ANNEN
EROTIC MUSEUM
MOLEN-STEEG
DE WAAG

To Anne Frank House
MAGNA PLAZA
NEW CHURCH
DAMRAK-STEEG
Dam (#4, #9, #16 & #24)
ST. ANNEN STR.
RED LIGHT DISTRICT
ST. JANS STR.
BLOEDSTR.
KORTE KONINGSSTR.

POST
ROYAL PALACE
Dam (#1, #2, #5 & #14)
Dam Square
NAT'L MONUMENT
burgwal
STOOF
BARNDESTG.
Nieuwmarkt
Nieuwmarkt
KEIZERSSTR.
ST. ANTONIESBREESTR.

Singel
PALEISSTR.
KEIZERSRIJK
NIEUWEZIJDS VOORBURGWAL
Dam (#14)
KALVERSTR.
PIJLSTG. DAMSTR.
HASH MUSEUM
Voor.
BETHANIEN-STRAAT
HOOGSTR.
KOVENIERSBURGWAL
DIJKSTRAAT

SPUISTRAAT
DE PAPEGAAI
SPAAR.
NES
ST. PIETERS-POORT
WIJDE LOMBARD-STEEG
Achterburgwal
burgwal
HOOGSTR.

AMSTERDAM MUSEUM
GALLERY
ROKIN
KUIPERS-STEEG
Spui (#9, #14, #16, & #24)
RUSLAND
AMST. UNIVERSITY
KOVENIERSBURGWAL
RAAMGRACHT
REMBRANDT'S HOUSE

BEGIJNHOF
Spui (#1, #2 & #5)
Spui Square
WATER-STEEG
GEO
TAKST.
GRIMBURGWAL
SLIJKSTR.
OUDEMAN-HUISPOORT
Kloveniersburgwal
VERVERSSTR.
FLEA MARKET
Waterlooplein

Singel
KALVERSTR.
HANDBOOG
VOETBOOG
ROKIN
Rederij P. Kooij
ALLARD-PIERSEN MUSEUM
VENDELSTR.
NIEUWE DOELENSTR.
STAALSTR.
Zwanenburgwal
OPERA HOUSE

KONINGSPLEIN
HEILIGEWEG
V&D DEPT. STORE
Muntplein (#4, #9, #14, #16 & #24)
STAALKADE
Amstel
Waterlooplein (#9 & #14)

Koningsplein (#1, #2 & #5)
FLOWER MARKET
SINGEL
KALVERTOREN MALL
MINT TOWER
FLOWER MARKET
Muntplein
REG.
HALVE-MAAN-STIG.
AMSTEL
AMSTEL

▲▲Amsterdam Museum

This creative museum works hard to make the city's history engaging and fun. The "DNA" section gives a quick overview. Then interactive exhibits help you follow the city's growth from fishing village to global trade center to Rembrandt (several paintings) to 1960s hippie haven, and the many challenges of the 21st century: housing, drug policy, prostitution, and immigration issues.

▸ *€10, open Mon-Fri 10:00-17:00, Sat-Sun 11:00-17:00, uncrowded place to buy Museumkaart, pleasant restaurant, located next to Begijnhof at Kalverstraat 92, tel. 020/523-1822, ahm.nl.*

✪ *For more on the museum and its free, portrait-lined pedestrian corridor, see page 25 of the Amsterdam City Walk chapter.*

▲▲Amstelkring Museum
(Our Lord in the Attic/Museum Ons' Lieve Heer op Solder)

For two centuries (1578-1795), Catholicism in Amsterdam was illegal but tolerated (like pot in the 1970s). Catholic churches were vandalized and Catholic kids were razzed on their way to school. Catholics were forbidden to worship openly, so they gathered secretly to say Mass in homes and offices.

Imagine the jubilation in 1663 when Our Lord in the Attic opened its doors. The church—embedded within a merchant's townhouse—was low-profile enough to appease the Protestant authorities but glorious enough to inspire the Catholic faithful.

Today, at the Amstelkring Museum, you can visit the church, as well as the merchant's apartments and servants' back house. Start with the...

Merchant's Apartments: The ornate Parlor (with a big fireplace) is where he entertained guests. In the Canal Room (with period furnishings), the family hung out and slept, sitting upright in small bed cabinets. Upstairs is...

The Church: The church is long and narrow, with an altar at one end, an organ at the other, and two balconies overhead to maximize the seating (150 worshippers) in this relatively small space. Compared with Amsterdam's whitewashed Protestant churches, this Catholic church has touches of elaborate Baroque decor, with statues of saints, garlands, and baby angels.

Look closely at the altar. The base of the left column—made of wood

The Amstelkring historic house with... ...a hidden Catholic church in the attic.

painted to look like marble—is hollow. Inside is a foldout wooden pulpit (nearby photos show how it worked).

Browse nearby rooms to see Catholic religious paraphernalia—a 400-year-old altar, a collection box (*voor St. Pieter*), a confessional, several gold monstrances—the kind of luxury, ostentation, and Catholic mumbo-jumbo that drove thrifty Calvinists nuts. Finish downstairs in...

The Back House: Like many townhomes, this had rooms at the back. You'll see two different kitchens, with blue tiles, yellow walls, and diffuse lighting from a skylight—straight out of a Vermeer painting.

▶ *€8, includes audioguide, open Mon-Sat 10:00-17:00, Sun and holidays 13:00-17:00, no photos, steep staircases, expect renovation until 2015, Oudezijds Voorburgwal 40, tel. 020/624-6604, opsolder.nl.*

▲▲Red Light District

Europe's most popular ladies of the night tease and tempt here, as they have for centuries, in streets surrounding the historic Old Church (Oude Kerk). The neighborhood also boasts sex shops, a sex museum, marijuana cafes, and a marijuana museum. It's liveliest and least seedy in the evening.

⊙ See the Red Light District Walk chapter.

Sex Museums

Amsterdam has two sex museums. While visiting one can be called sightseeing, visiting both is harder to explain.

The **Erotic Museum** in the Red Light District is five floors of uninspired paintings, videos, old photos, and sculpture (€7, not covered by

Museumkaart, open daily 11:00-late, at Oudezijds Achterburgwal 54, tel. 020/624-7303; ✪ see page 82).

The **Damrak Sex Museum** is cheaper and better. It tells the story of pornography from Roman times through 1960. Every sexual deviation is revealed. You'll see early French pornographic photos; memorabilia from Europe, India, and Asia; a Marilyn Monroe tribute; and some S&M displays (€4, not covered by Museumkaart, open daily 9:30-23:00, Damrak 18, a block from Central Station, tel. 020/622-8376).

West Amsterdam

Walking west from busy Dam Square, you quickly reach a quieter world of leafy streets along some of the city's grandest canals. Farther west is the residential Jordaan neighborhood.

▲▲▲Anne Frank House

Thirteen-year-old Anne and her family spent two years hiding in the back rooms of this townhouse during the Nazi occupation. The thoughtfully-designed exhibit covers the family's ordeal, Anne's famous diary, and the Holocaust.

✪ See the Anne Frank House Tour chapter.

Westerkerk

The landmark church has a barren interior, Rembrandt's body buried somewhere under the pews, and Amsterdam's tallest steeple, with a grand city view. To go up the tower, you must take a tour (first-come, first-served), so lines can be long.

▶ *The church interior is free and generally open April-Sept Mon-Sat 11:00-15:00, closed Sun and Oct-March. The tower is €7, with tours on the half-hour April-Sept Mon-Sat 10:00-18:00, July-Aug until 20:00; Oct Mon-Sat 11:00-16:00; last tour departs 30 minutes before closing, Nov-March tourable only by appointment—call 020/689-2565 or email anna@westertorenamsterdam.nl.*

Houseboat Museum (Woonbootmuseum)

In the 1930s, big modern cargo ships came into widespread use. The old, sail-powered cargo boats found new life as houseboats lining the canals of Amsterdam. Today, 2,500 such boats—their cargo holds turned into classy, comfortable living rooms—are called home. For a peek into this

Houseboat Museum with Captain Vincent   The Stedelijk has wild modern art.

gezellig (cozy) world, visit this tiny museum. Captain Vincent enjoys show-ing visitors around the houseboat, which feels lived-in because, until 1997, it was.

▶ *€3.75, not covered by Museumkaart; open March-Oct Tue-Sun 11:00-17:00, Nov-Dec and Feb Fri-Sun 11:00-17:00; on Prinsengracht, oppo-site #296 facing Elandsgracht, tel. 020/427-0750, houseboatmuseum.nl.*

Southwest Amsterdam

Three major museums dot the landscape of the large park called Museumplein. Several other interesting sights lie nearby, as well as recom-mended eateries. Everything is within a 5- to 10-minute walk. Trams #2 and #5 from Central Station drop you right there.

▲▲▲Rijksmuseum

This incomparable collection of 17th-century Dutch Masters is led by Rembrandt's brooding brown canvases, Vermeer's slice-of-life moments, Frans Hals' vivacious portraits, and Jan Steen's whimsical tableaux.

✪ See the Rijksmuseum Tour chapter.

▲▲▲Van Gogh Museum

The museum's 200 paintings offer a virtual stroll through the artist's work and life. Highlights include *Sunflowers, The Bedroom, The Potato Eaters,* and many penetrating self-portraits.

✪ See the Van Gogh Museum Tour chapter.

▲▲Stedelijk Museum

The Netherlands' top modern-art museum is fun, far-out, and refreshing.

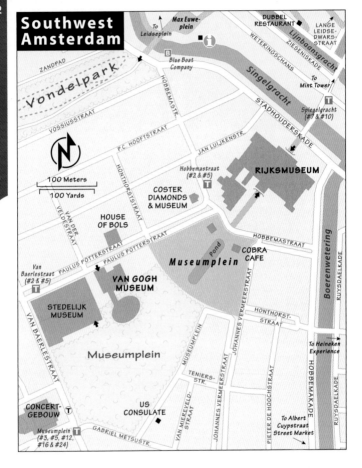

Southwest Amsterdam

ZANDPAD

Vondelpark

To Leidseplein

Max Euwe-plein

DUBBEL RESTAURANT

LANGE LEIDSE-DWARS-STRAAT

Lijnbaansgracht

WETERINGSCHANS

ZIESENISKADE

Blue Boat Company

Singelgracht

WETERINGSCHANS

To Mint Tower

VOSSIUSSTRAAT

HOBBEMASTR.

STADHOUDERSKADE

Spiegelgracht (#7 & #10)

P.C. HOOFTSTRAAT

JAN LUIJKENSTR.

100 Meters

100 Yards

HONTHORSTSTRAAT

Hobbemastraat (#2 & #5)

RIJKSMUSEUM

COSTER DIAMONDS & MUSEUM

VAN DER VELDESTRAAT

HOUSE OF BOLS

HOBBEMASTRAAT

Pond

COBRA CAFE

Boerenwetering

RUYSDAELKADE

Van Baerlestraat (#2 & #5)

PAULUS POTTERSTRAAT

PAULUS POTTERSTRAAT

Museumplein

VAN GOGH MUSEUM

STEDELIJK MUSEUM

Museumplein

HONTHORST-STRAAT

To Heineken Experience

MUSEUMPLEIN

JOHANNES VERMEERSTRAAT

HOBBEMAKADE

RUYSDAELKADE

VAN BAERLESTRAAT

TENIERS-STR.

VAN MIEREVELD-STRAAT

JOHANNES VERMEERSTRAAT

PIETER DE HOOCHSTRAAT

CONCERT-GEBOUW

US CONSULATE

To Albert Cuypstraat Street Market

Museumplein (#3, #5, #12, #16 & #24)

GABRIEL METSUSTR.

The collection includes post-1945 experimental and conceptual art as well as works by Picasso, Chagall, Cézanne, Kandinsky, and Mondrian. (Its specialty, though, is temporary exhibits on the cutting edge.) The Stedelijk (STAYD-eh-lik) boasts a newly spiffed-up building, which flaunts an architecturally daring entry facing Museumplein.

▶ *€15, open Tue-Wed 11:00-17:00, Thu 11:00-22:00, Fri-Sun 10:00-18:00, closed Mon, café with outdoor seating, top-notch shop, Paulus Potterstraat 13/Museumplein 10, tel. 020/573-2911, stedelijk.nl.*

▲Museumplein's Other Sights

Museumplein—a park-like square bordered by the Rijks, Van Gogh, Stedelijk, and the Concertgebouw (classical music hall)—is interesting even to art haters. Mimes, human statues, and crafts booths dot the square. Amsterdam's best acoustics are found underneath the Rijksmuseum, where street musicians perform everything from chamber music to Mongolian throat singing. Skateboarders career across a concrete tube, while locals enjoy a park bench or a coffee at the Cobra Café.

Nearby is **Coster Diamonds,** a handy place to see a diamond-cutting and polishing demo. Free, frequent, and interesting 30-minute tours are followed by a sales pitch (daily 9:00-17:00, Paulus Potterstraat 2, tel. 020/305-5555, costerdiamonds.com). Their Diamond Museum is worth the admission for most (€7.50, covered by Museumkaart, open daily 9:00-17:00, tel. 020/305-5300, diamantmuseumamsterdam.nl).

The **House of Bols: Cocktail & Genever Experience** is a fun self-guided walk through what is essentially an ad for Holland's leading distillery, culminating in a chance to taste up to five different local gins (€12.50, not covered by Museumkaart, open daily 12:00-17:30, until later Fri-Sat,

Museumplein—a people-friendly park

Heineken brewery—a frothy "experience"

last entry 45 minutes before closing, must be 18, Paulus Potterstraat 14, tel. 020/570-8575, houseofbols.com).

Heineken Experience

This famous brewery, having moved its operations to the suburbs, has converted its original headquarters into a slick, Disneyesque beerfest. There's a beer-making simulation ride, do-it-yourself music videos, wacky photo ops, and lots of hype about all things Heineken. It's fun, if overpriced.

▶ *€17, includes two drinks, open daily 11:00-19:00, last entry at 17:30; tram #16, #24, or #25 to Heinekenplein; an easy walk from Rijksmuseum, tel. 020/523-9222, heinekenexperience.com.*

▲▲Vondelpark

This huge, lively city park is popular with families, romantic couples, strolling seniors, and hippies sharing blankets and beers. It's a favored venue for free summer concerts. On a sunny afternoon, it's a hedonistic scene that seems to say, "Parents...relax."

Southern Canal Belt

This outer ring of canals lies south (and southwest) of the Old Center. The neighborhood's broad canals and classically gabled townhouses make it a pleasant and quiet area, speckled with a few small sights.

▲Willet-Holthuysen Museum (a.k.a. Herengracht Canal Mansion)

This 1687 townhouse is a must for devotees of Hummel-topped sugar bowls and Louis XVI-style wainscoting. For the rest of us, it's a pleasant look inside a typical (rich) home with much of the original furniture and

Vondelpark—paths, greenery, happy locals

Willet-Holthuysen—a historic mansion

The Netherlands

The word *Netherlands* means "lowlands." ("Holland" is just a nickname; North and South Holland are two of the country's 12 provinces.) The country occupies the low-lying delta near the mouth of three of Europe's large rivers, including the Rhine. In medieval times, inhabitants built a system of earthen dikes to protect their land from flooding caused by tides and storm surges. Today's 350 miles of dikes and levees are high-tech. Much of the Dutch landscape is reclaimed from the sea, rivers, and lakes.

The Netherlands is Europe's most densely populated country (16.7 million people, 1,200 people per square mile), and the average income is on a par with the US ($42,700). Though only 8 percent of the labor force is made up of farmers, 70 percent of the land is cultivated.

Several Dutch icons came directly from the country's flat, reclaimed landscape: Windmills and canals drained the land. Wooden shoes *(klompen)* allowed farmers to walk across soggy fields. Tulips and other flowers grew well in the sandy soil near dunes. All this technological tinkering with nature prompted a popular local saying: "God made the Earth, but the Dutch made Holland."

decor. Forget the history and just browse through a dozen rooms of beautiful (if saccharine) objects from the 19th century.

A ground-floor video explains how the wealthy heiress Louise Holthuysen and the art-collecting bon vivant Abraham Willet got married and became joined at the hyphen, then set out to make their home the social hub of Amsterdam.

You'll see their pre-electricity kitchen, their paintings of frolicking French nobles, and rooms of Louis XVI-style furniture. Imagine Abraham and Louise entertaining in the impressive gilded ballroom, then retiring to the dining room to eat off the 275-piece Meissen porcelain set, and finishing with tea in the garden room, gazing out at symmetrically curved hedges and classical statues. You'll even see the couple's bedroom, with a canopy bed and a chamber pot tucked beneath.

▶ *€8, open Mon-Fri 10:00-17:00, Sat-Sun 11:00-17:00, Herengracht 605, tel. 020/523-1822, willetholthuysen.nl.*

Rembrandtplein and Tuschinski Theater

One of the city's premier nightlife spots is the leafy Rembrandtplein (and surrounding streets and squares, especially Thorbeckeplein). On the square stands a fun 3-D statue group recreating Rembrandt's *Night Watch*. The nearby **Tuschinski Theater,** a movie palace from the 1920s (a half-block from Rembrandtplein at Reguliersbreestraat 26-28), glitters inside and out. The exterior design forces the round peg of Art Nouveau (Tiffany-style windows, curvy iron lamps) into the square hole of Art Deco. Inside, the lobby (free to enter) is sumptuous. The Tuschinski is a delightful old place to see first-run movies.

▶ *Trams #4, #9, and #14 go to Rembrandtplein.*

▲Leidseplein

Brimming with cafés, this people-watching mecca is an impromptu stage for street artists, jugglers, and unicyclists. At night, it hums.

⚙ For more on Leidseplein, see page 33 of the Amsterdam City Walk.

Small Niche Museums

Amsterdam has a number of small collections of niche-interest items, housed inside old mansions. These four museums can be a bit underwhelming (and overpriced), but they're worth a visit if you enjoy browsing, with low expectations.

Tassen Museum (Hendrikje Museum of Bags and Purses): This hardworking little museum fills an elegant 1664 canal house with 500 years of bag and purse history—from before the invention of pockets through the 20th century. It's all well-described in English. Start on the top floor, and don't miss the creative and surreal bag styles of the 1920s and 1930s (€8.50, daily 10:00-17:00, behind Rembrandtplein at Herengracht 573, tel. 020/524-6452, tassenmuseum.nl).

Pipe Museum (Pijpenkabinet): This quirky-yet-classy museum holds 300 years of pipes in a 17th-century canal house. (It's almost worth the admission price just to see the inside of one of these elegant homes.) The (free) street-level shop, Smokiana, sells new and antique pipes, various smoking curiosities, and scholarly books written by the shop's owner. If you pay admission, a docent will accompany you upstairs through a tour of smoking history: pre-Columbian terra-cotta pipes (from the discoverers of tobacco, dating from around 500 B.C.); intricate Baroque pipes; and miscellaneous Victorian smoking paraphernalia. Your guide can explain why some pipes are a foot long, or why the opium pipes have their bowls in the center of the stem (€8, Wed-Sat 12:00-18:00, closed Sun-Tue, tel. 020/421-1779, just off Leidsestraat at Prinsengracht 488, pijpenkabinet.nl).

The Canal House (Het Grachtenhuis): Though promoted as a way to experience a great canalside mansion, this is basically a series of empty rooms showing videos—interesting but pricey (€12, Tue-Sun 10:00-18:00, closed Mon, Herengracht 386, hetgrachtenhuis.nl).

Bijbels Museum: An old-school, uninspired jumble of all things Biblical, with temporary exhibits that'll disappoint most visitors (€8, Mon-Sat 10:00-17:00, Sun 11:00-17:00, Herengracht 366-368, tel. 020/624-2436, bijbelsmuseum.nl).

Southeast Amsterdam

Stretching from the edge of the Old City Center to the very outskirts, this neighborhood has a number of interesting sights, especially in the former Jewish Quarter. To reach the following sights from the train station, take tram #9 or #14. All of these sights (except the Tropical Museum) are close enough to be connected on foot—or, better yet, by bike.

Waterlooplein and the Jewish Quarter

Several sights cluster near the large square, Waterlooplein, which grew up near the former Jewish Quarter. Survey the neighborhood from the lamp-lined **Blauwbrug** ("Blue Bridge") over the Amstel River. It's at this point that the river's course is channeled to form the city's canals.

Scan clockwise. The big, curved, modern building is known as the **"Stopera,"** as it's the combo City Hall (stadhuis) and opera. Behind the Stopera (though not visible from the bridge) is the **Waterlooplein Flea Market.** Every day except Sunday, you'll find stalls selling cheap clothes, hippie stuff, old records, and tourist knickknacks.

To the right of the Stopera was the **former Jewish Quarter,** marked by the twin gray steeples of the Moses and Aaron Church. Since medieval times, Amsterdam had a thriving Jewish population. Jews, who were often outcasts in the rest of Europe, were welcome in this cosmopolitan city that cared more about business than religion. By 1940, one in ten Amsterdammers was Jewish, and most lived in this neighborhood. But during the Nazi occupation, Jews were rounded up and shipped to extermination camps in Eastern Europe. By war's end, more than 100,000

Southeast Amsterdam

of the country's 135,000 Jews had died. Today, about 25,000 Jews live in Amsterdam, and the Jewish Quarter has blended with the modern city.

Continue panning clockwise. The cute little **drawbridge,** while not famous, is certainly photogenic. Beyond that is the city-block-sized **Hermitage Amsterdam.** Crossing the Amstel upstream is the **Magere Brug** ("Skinny Bridge")—one of Amsterdam's best places to kiss.

▲Rembrandt's House (Museum Het Rembrandthuis)

A middle-aged Rembrandt lived here from 1639 to 1658 after his wife's death, as his popularity and wealth dwindled down to obscurity and bankruptcy. As you enter, ask when the next etching demonstration is scheduled and pick up the excellent audioguide.

Rembrandt's House has a modern entrance.

Gassan's free diamond-polishing demo

During your visit, you explore Rembrandt's reconstructed house, filled with exactly what his bankruptcy inventory of 1656 said he owned. Imagine him at work in his reconstructed studio. Marvel at his personal collection of exotic objects, many of which he included in paintings. At the etching demonstration, you learn about the etching process: drawing in soft wax on a metal plate that's then dipped in acid, inked up, and printed. For the finale, enjoy several rooms of original Rembrandt etchings. You're not likely to see a single painting, but the master's etchings are marvelous and well-described. I came away wanting to know more about the man and his art.

▶ €10, includes audioguide, open daily 10:00-17:00, etching demonstrations almost hourly, Jodenbreestraat 4, tel. 020/520-0400, rembrandt huis.nl.

▲Gassan Diamonds

This is one of many shops in this "city of diamonds" that offer free 15-minute tours, usually as part of a large tour group. You get to see experts behind magnifying glasses polishing the facets of precious diamonds, then visit an intimate sales room to see (and perhaps buy) a mighty shiny yet very tiny souvenir.

▶ Free, open daily 9:00-17:00, a block from Rembrandt's House at Nieuwe Uilenburgerstraat 173, tel. 020/622-5333, gassan.com, handy WC.

▲▲Hermitage Amsterdam

The famous Hermitage Museum in St. Petersburg, Russia loans part of its vast collection of art to Amsterdam. Amsterdam's Hermitage branch is the biggest of several in Europe, filling the Amstelhof, a 17th-century former nursing home that takes up a whole city block along the Amstel River.

The collection changes about every six months—check the museum's website to see what's on during your visit. Almost every show is a major arts event. The one small permanent "History Hermitage" exhibit explains the historic connection between the Dutch (Orange) and Russian (Romanov) royal families.

▸ *Generally €15, but price varies with exhibit. Open daily 10:00-17:00; come later in the day to avoid crowds. Mandatory free bag check, café. Located at Nieuwe Herengracht 14, tram #9 from the train station, recorded info tel. 020/530-7488, hermitage.nl.*

De Hortus Botanical Garden

A unique oasis of tranquility within the city, this large park is one of the oldest botanical gardens in the world, from 1638. As Dutch sailors roamed the globe, they returned with medicinal herbs, cacti, palm trees, and Europe's first coffee plant (brought from Ethiopia in 1706). Today, there are 6,000 different kinds of plants and several greenhouses (one for butterflies). No mobile phones are allowed, because "our collection of plants is a precious community—treat it with respect."

▸ *€7.50, not covered by Museumkaart, open daily 10:00-17:00, inviting Orangery Café serves tapas, Plantage Middenlaan 2A, tel. 020/625-9021, dehortus.nl.*

▲Jewish Historical Museum (Joods Historisch Museum)

The story of the Netherlands' Jews through three centuries also serves as a good introduction to Judaism and Jewish traditions. The collection spreads across four historic former synagogues that have been joined by steel and glass to make one modern complex.

The centerpiece of the museum is the **Great Synagogue.** Take a seat and picture it during its prime (1671-1943): men worshipping downstairs, women above in the gallery. On the east wall (the symbolic direction of Jerusalem) were the Torah scrolls. The raised platform in the center of the room is where the text was sung.

Video displays around the room explain Jewish customs, from birth (circumcision) to puberty (the bar/bat mitzvah, celebrating the entry into adulthood) to Passover celebrations to marriage—culminating in the groom stomping on a glass while everyone shouts "Mazel tov!"

A Torah at the Jewish Historical Museum

Dutch Theater, where Nazis imprisoned Jews

Next, head upstairs where exhibits trace the history of Amsterdam's Jews from 1600 to 1900. From here, a sky bridge leads to the **New Synagogue** and the 20th century, including sobering artifacts from the devastating Nazi occupation.

Find contemporary exhibits in the **Aanbouw Annex,** then finish your visit by crossing the street to the **Portuguese Synagogue.** Built in the 1670s, it survived World War II, and stands today as a big, open, and simple place of worship.

▶ *€12, more for special exhibits, ticket also covers Dutch Theater—see next listing. Open daily 11:00-17:00 (Portuguese Synagogue 10:00-16:00), last entry 30 minutes before closing. Kosher café. Located at Jonas Daniel Meijerplein 2, tel. 020/531-0310, jhm.nl.*

▲Dutch Theater (Hollandsche Schouwburg)

Once a lively theater in the Jewish neighborhood, this building served a notorious function during World War II—as a holding pen for local Jews rounded up and destined for Nazi concentration camps. Some 70,000 victims spent time here, awaiting transfer. On the wall, 6,700 family names pay tribute to 104,000 Jews deported and killed by the Nazis.

Upstairs is a small history exhibit with a model of the ghetto, plus photos and memorabilia (such as shoes and letters) of some victims, putting a human face on the staggering numbers. While the exhibit is small, it offers plenty to think about. Back in the ground-floor courtyard, notice the wooden tulips, where visiting school groups attach messages of hope.

▶ *Covered by €12 Jewish Historical Museum ticket, open daily 11:00-16:00, Plantage Middenlaan 24, tel. 020/531-0340, hollandscheschouwburg.nl.*

▲▲Dutch Resistance Museum (Verzetsmuseum)

Bam—it's May of 1940 and the Germans invade the Netherlands, pummel Rotterdam, drive Queen Wilhelmina into exile, and—in four short days of fighting—hammer home the message that resistance is futile.

This museum tells the rest of the story—how the Dutch survived under Nazi occupation from 1940 to 1945. They faced a timeless moral dilemma: Is it better to collaborate with a wicked system to effect small-scale change—or to resist outright, even if your efforts are doomed to fail? You'll learn why some chose the former, and others the latter.

You'll see propaganda movie clips, study forged ID cards under a magnifying glass, and read about ingenious and courageous efforts—big and small—to undermine the Nazi regime. Patriotic vandals turned Nazi V-for-Victory posters into W-for-Wilhelmina. Journalists circulated underground newspapers. Labor organizers ordered citywide strikes. Ordinary citizens hid radios under floorboards and Jews inside closets. They suffered through the "Hunger Winter" of 1944 to 1945, when 20,000 died. Finally, it was springtime, the Allies liberated the country, and Nazi helmets were turned into Dutch bedpans.

▶ *€8, includes audioguide. Open Tue-Fri 10:00-17:00, Sat-Mon 11:00-17:00, no flash photos, mandatory and free bag check, Plantage Kerklaan 61 (near Amsterdam's famous zoo). Tel. 020/620-2535, verzets museum.org.*

▲Tropical Museum (Tropenmuseum)

As close to the Third World as you'll get without lots of vaccinations, this imaginative museum offers wonderful re-creations of tropical life and explanations of Third World problems (largely created by Dutch colonialism and the slave trade). Ride the elevator to the top floor, and circle your way down through this immense collection, opened in 1926 to give the Dutch people a peek at their vast colonial holdings.

▶ *€10, open Tue-Sun 10:00-17:00, tram #9 to Linnaeusstraat 2, cafeteria serves tropical food, tel. 020/568-8200, tropenmuseum.nl.*

Northeast Amsterdam

Central Library (Openbare Bibliotheek Amsterdam)

This huge, striking, multistory building holds almost 1,400 seats—many with wraparound views of the city—and lots of Internet terminals and Wi-Fi

Dutch Resistance Museum makes you think.

NEMO's ship-shape science museum

(€1/30 minutes, sign up at the desk). Everything's relaxed and inviting, from the fun kids' zone and international magazine and newspaper section on the ground floor to the rooftop cafeteria, with its dramatic view (€10 meals, salad bar).

▶ *Free, open daily 10:00-22:00, a 10-minute walk east of Central Station, tel. 020/523-0900, oba.nl.*

NEMO (National Center for Science and Technology)

This kid-friendly science museum is a city landmark. The distinctive copper-green structure (by well-known Italian architect Renzo Piano) juts up from the water like a sinking ship, prompting critics to nickname it the *Titanic*. The many exhibits, both permanent and temporary, allow you to explore science by playing with bubbles, giant dominoes, and room-size pinball machines. The museum's motto: "It's forbidden NOT to touch!" There's a rooftop restaurant with a great city view.

▶ *€13.50, open June-Aug daily 10:00-17:00, Sept-May generally closed Mon. The roof terrace—open until 19:00 in the summer—is generally free. Located at Oosterdok 2, a 15-minute walk from Central Station, or take bus #22, #42, or #43 to the Kadijksplein stop. Tel. 020/531-3233, e-nemo.nl.*

▲▲Netherlands Maritime Museum (Nederlands Scheepvaartmuseum)

Given the Dutch seafaring heritage, this is an appropriately big and impressive place.

The east building holds the core collection: globes, an exhibit on the city's busy shipping port, original navigational tools, displays of ship ornamentation, and paintings of dramatic 17th-century naval battles against the

British. The west building has exhibits on whaling and of seafaring in the Dutch Golden Age.

Moored just outside is a replica of the *Amsterdam*, an 18th-century cargo ship of the Dutch East India Company (abbreviated VOC). Wander the decks, then duck your head and check out the captain and surgeon's quarters, and the hold. The ship is a little light on good historical information, but for naval buffs and *Pirates of the Caribbean* fans, the sight is plenty shipshape.

▶ *€15 covers both museum and ship, both open daily 9:00-17:00, bus #22 or #48 from Central Station to Kattenburgerplein 1, tel. 020/523-2222, scheepvaartmuseum.nl.*

▲EYE Film Institute Netherlands

This übersleek addition to the Amsterdam skyline is a film museum and cinema, located immediately across the water (the IJ) from Central Station. The EYE (a play on "IJ") is a complex of museum spaces, theaters for art films, special exhibits, shops, and a trendy waterside terrace café. Helpful attendants at the reception desk can get you oriented. Check the website for the schedule of events.

▶ *General entry is free, films cost €10, and exhibits cost around €10 (no cash accepted, but standard US credit cards OK), exhibits open 11:00-18:00, cinemas open daily at 10:00 until last screening (ticket office usually closes at 22:00 or 23:00), tel. 020/589-1400, eyefilm.nl.*

Getting There: *From the docks behind Central Station, catch the free ferry (labeled Buiksloterweg) across the river and walk left to IJpromenade 1.*

Day Trips

The Netherlands' efficient train system turns much of the country into a feasible day trip. Ask about "day return" tickets (same-day round trip) which are cheaper than two one-way tickets.

▲▲Haarlem

A half-hour away by train, the town of Haarlem is an agreeable mix of quaintness, history, and contemporary Dutch life.

The center of town is the massive main church, the **Grote Kerk.** Inside the church is Holland's largest organ (5,000 pipes) plus quirky exhibits like a replica of Foucault's pendulum and a 400-year-old cannonball.

In Haarlem, the main church anchors a town that's both quaint and contemporary.

A spacious square **(Grote Markt)** surrounds the church. Sip a coffee or beer at one of the cafés, and take in a view that's looked much the same for 700 years and been captured in well-known paintings. The square hosts colorful market days on Monday (clothing) and Saturday (general).

Haarlem is the hometown of Frans Hals, and the **Frans Hals Museum** has the world's largest collection of his work. Stand eye-to-eye with life-size, lifelike, warts-and-all portraits of Golden Age brewers, preachers, bureaucrats, and housewives. Most impressive are Hals' monumental group portraits.

The **Teylers Museum,** Holland's oldest, almost feels like a museum of a museum, with its well-preserved exhibits of skeletons, fossils, and primitive electronic gizmos.

Take in an expansive **view** of the countryside from the top of Haarlem's V&D Department store (at Grote Houtstraat 70). Finally (two blocks northeast of Grote Markt, off Lange Begijnestraat), you can stroll through quaint Haarlem's cozy little **Red Light District.**

▶ *Trains to Haarlem depart Amsterdam's Central Station every 30 minutes.*

From Haarlem's train station, the town center is a 10-minute walk—ask a local to point you to the "Grote Markt." There's a bike rental in the station. Avoid Haarlem on Mondays when many sights are closed. Haarlem's friendly TI (VVV) is in the town center at Verwulft 11 (toll tel. 0900-616-1600, haarlem.nl).

▲Other Dutch Destinations

The charming, canal-laced town of **Delft** (hometown of Vermeer and blue-painted ceramics) and its neighbor city, **The Hague,** make a rewarding day or two of sightseeing. **Arnhem** has the Arnhem Open-Air Folk Museum and the Kröller-Müller Museum of Van Gogh paintings (in Hogue Veluwe National Park). The **Historic Triangle** offers a nostalgic loop trip on a steam train and boat. **Keukenhof's** flower garden is one of the world's best (open in spring only).

If you want more, there's also **Edam** (an adorable village), **Alkmaar** (best on Friday for its cheese market), **Aalsmeer** (a bustling modern flower auction), **Schokland** (for a chance to walk on what was the bottom of the sea at this village/museum), open-air folk museums at **Enkhuizen** and **Zaanse Schans,** and more.

For more info on these places visit www.holland.com.

Sleeping

I've grouped my hotel listings into four neighborhoods: **West Amsterdam** (quiet canals, charming gabled buildings), **Central Amsterdam** (shopping and tourist sights, though a bit gritty), and Southwest Amsterdam's **Leidseplein** district (restaurants and nightlife while still cozy) and **Museumplein** area (a semi-suburban neighborhood).

I like hotels that are clean, central, good-value, friendly, run with a respect for Dutch traditions, and small enough to have a hands-on owner and stable staff. Four of these six virtues means it's a keeper. Double rooms listed in this book average around €110 (including a private bathroom). They range from a low of roughly €60 (very simple, with toilet and shower down the hall) to €260 (maximum plumbing and more).

Book as far in advance as possible, as Amsterdam is busy from mid-March to October.

A Typical Amsterdam Hotel Room

A typical €110 double room in Amsterdam will be small by American standards. It will have one double bed (either queen-sized or slightly narrower) or two twins. There's probably a bathroom in the room with a toilet, sink, and bathtub or shower. The room has a telephone and TV, and may have a safe. Single rooms, triples, and quads will have similar features.

Many of my listings are in old townhouses, decorated with charming old furniture. These might be somewhat creaky, have very steep stairs, and no elevator. Many hoteliers prefer cash and some will charge more for credit cards.

Breakfast—often included in the room price—is normally a self-service buffet of fresh bread, cereal, ham, cheese, yogurt, juice, and coffee or tea.

The hotel will have Internet access, either Wi-Fi or a public terminal in the lobby. At many of my listings, at least one of these options is free. The staff speaks English.

Making Reservations

Reserve as far in advance as you can, particularly if you'll be traveling during peak season (late March-Oct). Especially busy are late March to May (tulips in bloom), summer weekends, September (conventions), and some national holidays (e.g., King's Day in late April). Make reservations by phone, through the hotel's website, or with an email that reads something like this:

Dear Hotel Tulip,

I would like to reserve a double room for 2 people for 3 nights, arriving 19 July and departing 22 July. If possible, I would like a quiet room with a double bed (not twin beds), a canal view, and a shower (not a tub). Please let me know if you have a room available and the price. Thank you.

If they require your credit-card number for a deposit, you can send it by email (I do), but it's safer via phone, the hotel's secure website, or split between two emails. Once your room is booked, print out the confirmation, and reconfirm your reservation with a phone call or email a day or two in advance (alert them if you'll be arriving after 17:00). If canceling a reservation, some hotels require advance notice—otherwise they may bill you. Even if there's no penalty, it's polite to give at least three days' notice.

Hotel Price Code

$$$	Most rooms are €140 or more.
$$	Most rooms between €80-140.
$	Most rooms €80 or less.

These rates are for a standard double room with bath during high season; most don't include the city's 6 percent room tax. Verify the hotel's current rates online or by email. For the best prices, book direct.

Budget Tips

To get the best rates, book directly with the hotel, not through a hotel-booking engine. Start with the hotel's website, looking for promo deals. Check rates every few days, as prices can vary greatly based on demand. Email several hotels to ask for their best price and compare offers—you may be astonished at the range. Some may give a discount if you stay at least three nights or pay in cash.

Besides hotels, there are cheaper alternatives. Bed-and-breakfasts (B&Bs) offer a personal touch at a fair price—I've listed several. I also list a few all-ages hostels, which offer €25-30 dorm beds (and a few inexpensive doubles) and come with curfews and other rules. Airbnb.com makes it reasonably easy to find a place to sleep in someone's home.

Renting an apartment can save money if you're traveling as a family, staying more than a week, and planning to cook your own meals. Try homeaway.com (offering a wide range of listings) or vrbo.com (putting you directly in touch with owners).

Don't be too cheap when picking a place to stay. Anything under €100 (even my listings) can be a little rough around the edges. Choose a nice, central neighborhood. Construction noise is common in always-renovating Amsterdam, so consider asking for a quiet room in back. Your Amsterdam experience will be more memorable with a welcoming oasis to call home.

Sleeping

WEST AMSTERDAM: Tree-lined canals, gabled buildings, and candlelit restaurants; just minutes on foot to Dam Square. Many of my hotels are old mansions—charming but with lots of steep stairs.

$$$ The Toren Keizersgracht 164 tel. 020/622-6033, thetoren.nl	Chandeliered historic mansion by peaceful canal, classy yet friendly, elevator, ask about Rick Steves discount
$$$ Hotel Ambassade Herengracht 341 tel. 020/555-0222, ambassade-hotel.nl	Elegant and fresh, palatial public areas, top-notch staff, air-con, elevator, ask about Rick Steves discount
$$ Hotel Brouwer Singel 83 tel. 020/624-6358, hotelbrouwer.nl	Woody and old-timey, tranquil yet central, canal views, elevator, reserve way ahead
$$ Hotel Hoksbergen Singel 301 tel. 020/626-6043, hotelhoksbergen.com	Welcoming, well-run, peaceful canalside location, hands-on owners
$ Frederic Rent-a-Bike & Guestrooms Brouwersgracht 78 tel. 020/624-5509, frederic.nl	Various private rooms on gorgeous canal, from dumpy to elegant (see website), no breakfast
$$$ Wiechmann Hotel Prinsengracht 328-332 tel. 020/626-3321, hotelwiechmann.nl	Spacious, sparsely furnished dark-wood rooms, cozy public areas, Old World charm, canal views
$$ Hotel Hegra Herengracht 269 tel. 020/623-7877, hotelhegra.nl	Nine cozy rooms in old canalside townhouse
$ The Shelter Jordan Bloemstraat 179 tel. 020/624-4717, shelter.nl	90-bed hostel, bunk beds in dorms, friendly, Christian-run, near Anne Frank House
$$ Hotel Chic & Basic Amsterdam Herengracht 13 tel. 020/522-2345, chicandbasic.com	Boutique hotel, mod utilitarian design, young clientele, quiet neighborhood near Central Station
$$ Hotel Van Onna Bloemgracht 104 tel. 020/626-5801, hotelvanonna.nl	Simple industrial-strength rooms (no TV), leafy canal views, cozy attic rooms
$$ Maes B&B Herenstraat 26, tel. 020/427-5165 bedandbreakfastamsterdam.com	Great value, tastefully cozy and antique-filled, use of kitchen, warm hosts

$$ Herengracht 21 B&B Herengracht 21 tel. 020/625-6305, mobile 06-2812-0962 herengracht21.nl	Two stylish, intimate rooms in art-filled canal house, lovely host
$$ Sunhead of 1617 B&B Herengracht 152 mobile 06-2865-3572, sunhead.com	Four thoughtfully decorated flower-filled rooms, great breakfast, memorable owner Carlos
$$ Truelove Guesthouse Prinsenstraat 4 tel. 020/320-2500, mobile 06-2480-5672 cosyandwarm-amsterdam.com	Room-rental service rents homey furnished apartments with kitchens

CENTRAL AMSTERDAM: Ideal for shopping, tourist sights, and public transportation. But the area has traffic noise and urban grittiness, and the hotels can lack character.

$$$ Hotel Résidence Le Coin Nieuwe Doelenstraat 5 tel. 020/524-6800, lecoin.nl	42 bigger-than-average rooms with kitchenettes, near Mint Tower
$$$ Hotel Ibis Amsterdam Centre Stationsplein 49 tel. 020/522-2899, ibishotel.com	Huge modern place by Central Station, full comfort but no charm, drop-ins might score great deals
$$ Boogaard's B&B Pieter Jacobszstraat 21 mobile 06-3499-1941, boogaardsbnb.com	Delightful pad on narrow lane, run generously by American-born Peter, book early
$ Hotel Pax Raadhuisstraat 37 tel. 020/624-9735, hotelpax@tiscali.nl	11 plain but airy rooms with Ikea furniture, some w/o private bath
$ Hotel Aspen Raadhuisstraat 31 tel. 020/626-6714, hotelaspen.nl	Great budget value, 8 tidy stark rooms, kind-hearted managers
$ The Shelter City Barndesteeg 21 tel. 020/625-3230, shelter.nl	Hostel in Red-Light District, well-run and safe, evening Bible study

LEIDSEPLEIN: Mom-and-pop B&B-style coziness within a five-minute walk of restaurants and rowdy nightlife. Walk or easy tram to the center of town or Museumplein.

$$ Hotel de Leydsche Hof Leidsegracht 14 tel. 020/638-2327, mobile 06-5125-8588 freewebs.com/leydschehof	B&B, hidden gem, large white rooms, views of canal or leafy yard, lots of stairs, friendly owners

$$ Wildervanck B&B Keizersgracht 498 tel. 020/623-3846, wildervanck.com	Family-run, two tasteful rooms in an elegant old canal house, pleasant breakfast room
$$ Hotel Keizershof Keizersgracht 618 tel. 020/622-2855, hotelkeizershof.nl	Wonderfully Dutch, small-town charm, bright airy rooms, enthusiastic hospitality

MUSEUMPLEIN: Semi-suburban neighborhood within walking distance of Vondelpark and the Rijksmuseum. Good-value modern accommodations (elevators) but less Old World charm. Trams #1, #2, #5 to/from Central Station.

$$$ Hotel Piet Hein Vossiusstraat 51-53 tel. 020/662-7205, hotelpiethein.nl	81 stylishly sleek rooms, some air-con, swanky lounge, pleasant garden, quiet street
$$$ Hotel Fita Jan Luijkenstraat 37 tel. 020/679-0976, fita.nl	15 bright rooms, 100 yards from Van Gogh Museum, outdated décor but many amenities, free laundry service, warm welcome
$$ Hotel Filosoof Anna v.d.Vondelstraat 6 tel. 020/683-3013, hotelfilosoof.nl	Small rooms but uplifting atmosphere (classical music, philosophical theme rooms, garden)
$$ Hotel Alexander Vondelstraat 44-46 tel. 020/589-4020, hotelalexander.nl	32 modern rooms on quiet street, some overlook garden patio
$ Stayokay Vondelpark (IYHF) Zandpad 5 tel. 020/589-8996, stayokay.com	Hostel in Vondelpark, 500 beds, €20-40 dorm beds, €60-100 doubles (reserve well ahead), over-25s feel welcome
$$ Tulips B&B Sloterkade 65, tel. 020/679-2753 bedandbreakfastamsterdam.net	Cozy and bright rooms, some on a canal, friendly husband-wife owners, no elevator
$$ Hotel Hestia Roemer Visscherstraat 7 tel. 020/618-0801, hotel-hestia.nl	Safe street, efficient and family-run, 18 clean, airy, spacious rooms
$$ Hotel Parkzicht Roemer Visscherstraat 33 tel. 020/618-1954, parkzicht.nl	13 big, plain, old-fashioned rooms, steep stairs, some street noise

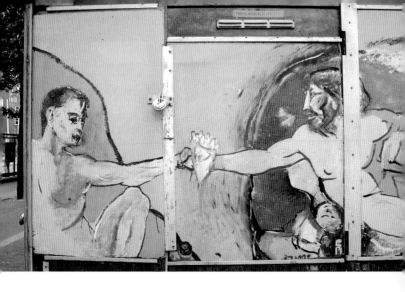

Eating

Amsterdam's thousand-plus eateries make for a buffet of dining options. Choose from elegant candlelit restaurants, an exotic Indonesian *rijsstafel*, a light meal outdoors alongside a canal, or stopping by a take-out stand for "Flemish" fries with mayonnaise. Besides meals, the Dutch spend endless hours sitting and drinking at outdoor cafés. Budget some money—and time—to sightseeing for your palate.

My listings are in Amsterdam's atmospheric neighborhoods, handy to recommended hotels and sights. Most are in West Amsterdam (near the Anne Frank House and the Jordaan—the most charming place to dine), Central Amsterdam (around Dam Square, Spui, and the Mint Tower), and Southwest Amsterdam (close to museums and recommended hotels).

No matter where you dine, expect it to be *gezellig*—a much-prized Dutch virtue, meaning an atmosphere of relaxed coziness.

Restaurant Price Code

$$$	Most main courses €18 or more
$$	Most main courses €12-18.
$	Most main courses €12 or less.

Based on the average price of a main dish on the menu. Salads and appetizers are several euros cheaper. So a typical meal at a $$ restaurant—including appetizer, main dish, house wine, water, and service—would cost about €30.

When in Amsterdam…

When in Amsterdam, I eat on the Dutch schedule. For breakfast, I eat at the hotel (bread, meat, cheese, egg) or grab a pastry and coffee at a café. Lunch (12:00-14:00) is a simple sandwich *(broodje)* or soup. In between meals, I might stop at a take-out stand for french fries *(friets)* or a pick-led herring. In the late afternoon, Amsterdammers enjoy a beverage with friends at an outdoor table on a lively square. Dinner (18:00-21:00) is the biggest meal of the day, the time for slowing down and savoring a multi-course restaurant meal.

Restaurants

As English is spoken everywhere, and the Dutch take an elegant-but-casual approach to dining, there's no need to learn a lot of special Dutch etiquette. Tipping is not necessary (because a 12-15 percent service charge is usually included in the menu price), but a tip of about 5-10 percent is a nice reward for good service. The Dutch are willing to pay for bottled water with their meal (Spa brand is popular, sparkling or still), but free tap water is always available upon request. All Dutch eateries are now non-smoking.

Cafés and Bars

Besides full-service restaurants, there are other places to fill the tank. An *eetcafé* is a simple restaurant serving meat-and-potatoes fare in a no-nonsense setting. A *salon de thé* serves tea and coffee, but also pastries and sandwiches.

Cafés are all-purpose establishments, serving light meals at mealtimes and coffee, drinks, and snacks the rest of the day. At night, cafes are essentially "bars," catering to the drinking crowd. *Bruin* cafés ("brown cafés") have a more traditional wood-paneled ambience. A "coffeeshop" is the code word for a café where marijuana is sold and consumed, though most offer drinks and munchies, too.

Cafés and bars with outdoor tables generally do not charge more if you sit outside (unlike in France or Italy). When ordering drinks in a café or bar, you can just pay as you go (especially if the bar is crowded), or wait until the end to settle up, as many locals do. If you get table service, take the cue from your waiter. There's no need to tip if you order at the counter, but if you get table service, it's nice to round up to the next euro ("keep the change").

Most cafés have a light-fare menu of sandwiches, salads, and soups, but some offer more ambitious meals. Throughout the day they cater to customers who just want to relax over a drink.

The Dutch love their coffee, enjoying many of the same drinks (espresso, cappuccino) served in American or Italian coffee shops. A *koffie verkeerd* (fer-KEERT, "coffee wrong") is an espresso with a lot of steamed milk. Many cafés/bars have a juicer for making fresh-squeezed orange juice, and they'll have the full array of soft drinks.

Order "a beer," and you'll get a *pils*—a light pilsner-type beer in a 10-ounce glass with a thick head leveled off with a stick. Typical brands are Heineken, Grolsch, Oranjeboom, and Amstel. Belgian beers are also popular.

The Dutch enjoy a chilled shot of *jenever* (yah-NAY-ver), a Dutch gin made from juniper berries. *Jong* (young) is sharper; *oude* (old) is mellow and more expensive. You'll find a variety of local fruit brandies and cognacs. The Dutch people drink a lot of fine wine, but it's almost all imported.

A quarter of Dutch people smoke tobacco. Holland has a long tradition as a smoking culture, being among the first to import the tobacco plant from the New World. Healthy, tanned, sixty-something Dutch people sip their beer, take a drag, and ask me why Americans murder themselves with Big Macs. Nevertheless, Dutch law has outlawed smoking tobacco almost everywhere indoors: restaurants, cafés and bars...and even marijuana-dealing coffeeshops.

Picnicking

Amsterdam makes it easy to turn a picnic into a first-class affair. Grab something to go and enjoy a bench in a lively square or with canal-side ambience.

Sandwiches *(broodjes)* of delicious cheese or ham on fresh bread are cheap at snack bars and delis. You'll find take-out stands selling herring, french fries, and ethnic foods.

Albert Heijn grocery stores (daily 8:00-22:00) have great deli sections with picnic-perfect take-away salads and sandwiches. There are handy locations near Dam Square, the Mint Tower, and inside Central Station (find them on the map on page 153).

Traditional Dutch Cuisine

Traditional Dutch cooking is basic and hearty—meat or fish, soup, fresh bread, boiled potatoes, cooked vegetables, and salad. Mashed potato dishes (*stamppot* or *hutspot*) served with meat and vegetables is classic Dutch comfort food. But these days, many Dutch people have traveled and become more sophisticated, enjoying dishes from around the world.

The Dutch are better known for their informal foods. Pickled herring (*haring*) come with onions or pickles on a bun. French fries (*Vlaamse friets*) are eaten with mayonnaise rather than ketchup. Popular Dutch cheeses are Edam (covered with red wax) or Gouda (HHHOW-dah). *Kroketten* (cro-quettes) are log-shaped rolls of meats and vegetables (kind of like corn dogs) breaded and deep-fried. *Pannenkoeken* (pancakes) can be either sweet dessert pancakes or crêpe-like, savory pancakes eaten as a meal.

Eating

For dessert, try *pannenkoeken, poffertjes* (small, sugared puffy pancakes), *stroopwafels* (syrup waffles), and *appelgebak* or *appeltaart* (apple pie).

Ethnic

Since its Golden Age days as a global trader, Amsterdam has adopted food from other lands.

Indonesian *(Indisch)*, from this former Dutch colony, is commonly served as a *rijsttafel* (literally, "rice table"), a multi-dish sampler of many spicy dishes and rice or noodles. A *rijsttafel* can be split between two hungry tourists. Various other menu items *(nasi rames, bami goring, nasi goring)* are also multi-dish meals. Common Indonesian sauces are peanut, red chili *(sambal)*, and dark soy.

You'll find Middle Eastern *shoarma* (roasted lamb in pita bread), falafel, gyros, or a *döner kebab*.

Surinamese *(Surinaamse)*, from the former colony on the northeast coast of South America, is a mix of Caribbean and Indonesian influences. The signature dish is *roti* (spiced chicken wrapped in a tortilla) and rice (white or fried) served with meats in sauces (curry and spices).

Alstublieft: Wherever you eat in Amsterdam—at fine restaurants, dim cafes, or the pickled herring shack—you'll constantly hear servers saying *"Alstublieft"* (AHL-stoo-bleeft). It's a useful, catchall polite word, meaning "please," "here's your order," "enjoy," and "you're welcome." You can respond by saying, *"Dank u wel"* (dahnk yoo vehl)—thank you.

CENTRAL AMSTERDAM: Eateries along the spine of the old center, from Central Station to Dam Square to the Mint Tower (see map, pages 152-153)

❶	**$$ Restaurant Kantjil en de Tijger** Spuistraat 291 tel. 020/620-0994	Indonesian, thriving and noisy, good-value *rijsttafel*, reservations smart (daily 12:00-23:00)
❷	**$ Kantjil to Go** Nieuwezijds Voorburgwal 342 tel. 020/620-3074)	Indonesian take-out bar, split a large box on Spui Square for delicious cheap meal (daily 12:00-23:00)
❸	**$ Café 't Gasthuys** Grimburgwal 7 tel. 020/624-8230	Brown café on canal, busy dumbwaiter cranks out light lunches and OK dinners (daily 11:00-16:30 & 17:30-22:00)
❹	**$$ De Jaren Café** Nieuwe Doelenstraat 20-22 tel. 020/625-5771	Modern, chic, and inviting; upstairs restaurant (w/salad bar), downstairs café (light lunch or drink), view deck (daily 9:30-23:00)
❺	**$ Pannenkoekenhuis Upstairs** Grimburgwal 2 tel. 020/626-5603	For pancakes, tiny characteristic perch up steep stairs (Mon-Fri 12:00-19:00, Sat 12:00-18:00, Sun 12:00-17:00)
❻	**$ La Place** Kalverstraat 203 tel. 020/622-0171	Fresh and appealing cafeteria at V&D dept. store (Sun-Mon 11:00-19:00, Tue-Wed 10:00-19:30, Thu-Sat 10:00-21:00)
❼	**$ Atrium University Cafeteria** Oudezijds Achterburgwal 237 tel. 020/525-3999	Ultra-cheap student cafeteria serves anyone (Mon-Fri 11:00-15:00 & 17:00-19:30, closed Sat-Sun)
❽	**$$$ Brasserie Restaurant de Roode Leeuw** Damrak 93-94 tel. 020/555-0666	Peaceful oasis for traditional Dutch food, overpriced and touristy but good service, reserve window seat (daily 12:00-22:00)
❾	**$ Dam Café** Dam 1 tel. 088-245-9080	At De Bijenkorf dept. store, salads and sandwiches, peaceful views of busy Damrak (Sun-Mon 11:00-20:00, Tue-Sat 10:00-20:00, Thu-Fri until 21:00)
❿	**$ Stubbe's Haring** Singel, 1013 GA Tel. 020/623-3212	Traditional take-out herring sandwiches from well-established place (Tue-Fri 10:00-18:00, Sat 10:00-17:00)

Eating

⑪	**$ Albert Heijn Supermarkets** Nieuwezijds Voorburgwal 226; Koningsplein 4; at Central Station	Grocery stores with good deli sections handy for picnics, no US credit cards (daily 8:00-22:00)

WEST AMSTERDAM: Charming canals near the Anne Frank House and Jordaan residential neighborhood (see map, pages 152-153)

⑫	**$$$ Restaurant de Luwte** Leliegracht 26-28 tel. 020/625-8548	Romantic, candlelit but modern, on picturesque street by canal, French Mediterranean cuisine (daily 18:00-22:00)
⑬	**$$ De Bolhoed** Prinsengracht 60 tel. 020/626-1803	Serious vegetarian and vegan, colorful setting, big splittable portions (daily 12:00-22:00)
⑭	**$$$ Café Restaurant de Reiger** Nieuwe Leliestraat 34 tel. 020/624-7426	Bistro ambience, classic Jordaan scene, fresh fish and French-Dutch cuisine, crowded late (Tue-Sun 17:00- 24:00, closed Mon)
⑮	**$ Café 't Smalle** Egelantiersgracht 12 tel. 020/623-9617	Simple light lunches, Belgian beer, good wine, canalside deck (daily 10:00-24:00)
⑯	**$$ Thai Fusion** Berenstraat 8 tel. 020/320-8332	Top-quality Thai in sleekly modern room in the Nine Little Streets (daily 16:30-22:30)
⑰	**$$ Toscana Italian Restaurant** Haarlemmerstraat 130 tel. 020/622-0353	Jordaan favorite for no-nonsense Italian, including pizza, in woody beer- hall setting (Sun-Wed 16:00-23:30, Thu-Sat 12:00-23:30)
⑱	**$$ Winkel** Noordermarkt 43 tel. 020/623-0223	Easygoing cornerside hangout, Euro-Dutch meals outside or in, great *appeltaart* (daily 8:00-late)
⑲	**$ Sara's Pancake House** Raadhuisstraat 45 tel. 020/320-0662	Basic diner, hardworking Sara cranks out sweet and savory organic flapjacks (daily until 22:30)
⑳	**$$$ Restaurant 't Stuivertje** Hazenstraat 58 tel. 020/623-1349	Small and family-run, French- inspired Dutch cuisine, elegant but unpretentious (Wed-Sun 17:30-22:00, closed Mon-Tue)
㉑	**$$$ Ristorante Toscanini** Lindengracht 75 tel. 020/623-2813	Up-market Italian, lively and always packed, reserve or arrive by 18:00 (Mon-Sat 18:00-22:30, closed Sun)

㉒	**$$ Villa Zeesicht** Torensteeg 7 tel. 020/626-7433	Classic European café at Torensluis bridge, so-so menu but great appeltaart and people-watching (daily 9:00-21:30)
㉓	**$ Café 't Papeneiland** Prinsengracht at #2 tel. 020/624-1989	For drinks only (no meals), classic old brown café with canal views, not for tourists (daily)
SOUTHWEST AMSTERDAM: Near Museumplein, Vondelpark, and Leidseplein (see map, pages 152-153)		
㉔	**$-$$$ "Restaurant Row"** Lange Leidsedwarsstraat	Various eateries of every price and cuisine, on street near Leidseplein
㉕	**$$ Restaurant Dubbel** Lijnbaansgracht 256 tel. 020/620-0909	Near touristy Leidseplein, good-value steak, fish, and veggies, friendly and somewhat local (daily 17:00-24:00)
㉖	**$ Restaurant Bazar** Albert Cuypstraat 182 tel. 020/675-0544	Fun and cheap Middle Eastern, lively and youthful setting (Mon-Fri 11:00-late, Sat-Sun 9:00-late).

Eating

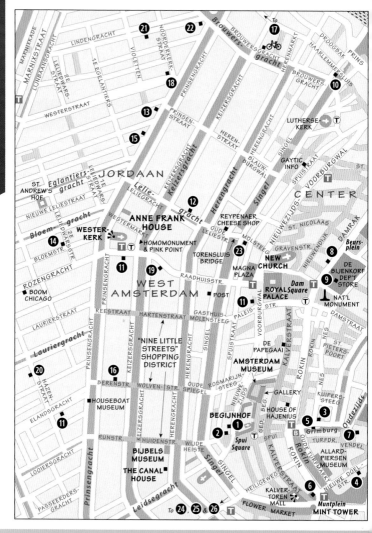

Amsterdam Restaurants

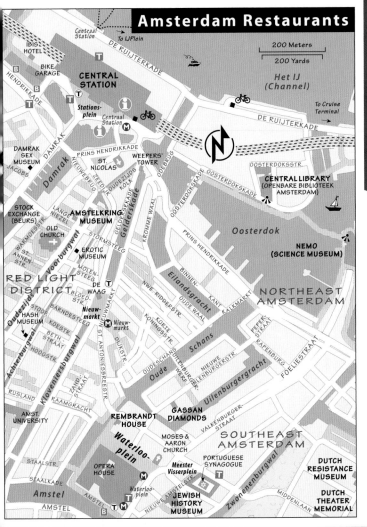

200 Meters

200 Yards

IBIS HOTEL

BIKE GARAGE

CENTRAL STATION

Stations-plein

Centraal Station

HENDRIKKADE

DE RUIJTERKADE

Centraal Station

To IJPlein

Het IJ (Channel)

To Cruise Terminal

DE RUIJTERKADE

DAMRAK SEX MUSEUM

JACOBS

DAMRAK

PRINS HENDRIKKADE

NIEUWEBRUG

ST. NICOLAS

ZEEDIJK

OUDEZIJDS KOLK

GELDERSEKADE

WEEPERS' TOWER

OUDEZIJDS

OPENBRUG

OOSTERDOKSKADE

OOSTERDOKSSTR.

CENTRAL LIBRARY (OPENBARE BIBLIOTHEEK AMSTERDAM)

STOCK EXCHANGE (BEURS)

OLD CHURCH

LANGE NIEZEL

AMSTELKRING MUSEUM

ST. ANNEN-STR.

WARMOES

VOORBURGWAL

STORMSTEEG

EROTIC MUSEUM

KROMME WAAL

OOSTERDOKSKADE

PRINS HENDRIKKADE

Oosterdok

NEMO (SCIENCE MUSEUM)

RED LIGHT DISTRICT

Oudezijds

ACHTERBURGWAL

HASH MUSEUM

STOOF

BARNDESTEEG

KOESTR.

BETH. STRAAT

MOLEN-STEEG

DE WAAG

Nieuw-markt

Nieuw-markt

BLOED-STR.

NWE RIDDERSTR.

Binnen

OUDE WAAL

Ellandsgracht

KANT

KALKMARKT

NORTHEAST AMSTERDAM

RUSLAND

HOOGSTR.

Kloveniersburgwal

ZAND-STRAAT

RAAMGRACHT

ST. ANTONIESBREESTR.

DIJKSTR.

KORTE KONINGSSTR.

OUDESCHANS

Schans

Oude

JONKER-BURG.

NIEUWE UILENBURGERSTR.

Uilenburgergracht

RAPENBURG

PEPER-STRAAT

FOELIESTRAAT

AMST. UNIVERSITY

STAALSTR.

REMBRANDT HOUSE

Waterloo-plein

OPERA HOUSE

STAALKADE

Amstel

AMSTEL

Waterloo-plein

GASSAN DIAMONDS

MOSES & AARON CHURCH

Meester Visserplein

JEWISH HISTORY MUSEUM

VALKENBURGER-STRAAT

PORTUGUESE SYNAGOGUE

SOUTHEAST AMSTERDAM

NIEUWE AMSTELSTR.

Zwanenburgwal

MIDDENLAAN

DUTCH RESISTANCE MUSEUM

DUTCH THEATER MEMORIAL

Practicalities

PLANNING

Amsterdam's best travel months—also the busiest and most expensive for flights and hotels—are late March through September. In spring, the weather is cool, but the nearby tulip fields are flowering, drawing surprisingly big crowds that drive up Amsterdam hotel prices. Summer brings the best weather (it's rarely too hot) and equally big crowds. In September, Amsterdam hosts seasonal conferences (again, drawing crowds). Amsterdam in winter is cold and rainy, but the crowds are fewer, cafés are cozy, and the city feels lively but not touristy.

Make sure your passport is up to date (to renew, see travel.state.gov). Call your debit- and credit-card companies about your plans. Book hotel rooms well in advance, especially for peak season (late March-Sept) and three-day holiday weekends (find a list at iamsterdam.com). Consider buying travel insurance. To avoid long lines, consider getting advance tickets (especially in peak season) for the Rijksmuseum, Van Gogh Museum, and Anne Frank House. If you're traveling beyond Amsterdam, research railpasses, train reservations, and car rentals.

Helpful Websites

Amsterdam Tourist Information: iamsterdam.com
The Netherlands' Tourist Information: holland.com.
Passports and Red Tape: travel.state.gov
Cheap Flights: kayak.com (for international flights), skyscanner.com
(for flights within Europe)
Airplane Carry-on Restrictions: tsa.gov
European Train Schedules: bahn.com
General Travel Tips: ricksteves.com (helpful info on train travel,
railpasses, car rental, travel insurance, packing lists, and much
more—plus updates to this book)

MONEY

The Netherlands uses the euro currency: 1 euro (€1) = about $1.30. To convert euros to dollars add about 30 percent: €20 = about $26, €50 = about $65. (Check oanda.com for the latest exchange rates.)

Withdraw money from an ATM (known as a *geldautomaat* in the Netherlands) using a debit card, just like at home. Visa and MasterCard are commonly used throughout Europe. Before departing, call your bank or credit-card company: Ask about international transaction fees, and alert them that you'll be making withdrawals in Europe. Many travelers bring a second debit/credit card as a backup. Many Amsterdam merchants prefer cash, and some places—even major grocery stores—won't accept foreign credit cards at all, so withdraw large amounts (€250-300) from the ATM.

While American magnetic-stripe credit cards are accepted almost everywhere in Europe, they may not work in some automated payment machines (e.g., ticket kiosks) geared for European-style chip-and-pin cards. Be prepared to pay with cash, try entering your card's PIN, or find a nearby cashier.

To keep your cash and valuables safe, wear a money belt. But if you do lose your credit or debit card, report the loss immediately with a phone call: Visa (tel. 303/967-1096), MasterCard (tel. 636/722-7111), and American Express (tel. 336/393-1111).

Practicalities

ARRIVAL IN AMSTERDAM

Amsterdam's Schiphol Airport

Schiphol (SKIP-pol) is very user-friendly. Though it officially has four terminals, it's really just one big building. You could walk it end to end in about 20 minutes. All terminals have ATMs, banks, shops, bars, and free Wi-Fi. For airport information, call toll tel. 0900-0141 (from other countries dial +31-20-794-0800), or visit schiphol.nl (airport code: AMS).

Baggage-claim areas for all terminals empty into the same arrival zone, called Schiphol Plaza. Here you'll find a busy TI (near Terminal 2, daily 7:00-22:00), a train station, and stops for buses heading into the city. Service Point (near Terminal 4) sells SIM cards, has an ATM, and ships packages. The "Train Tickets and Services" counter (near Burger King) provides all sorts of train ticket and info services without the long lines of Amsterdam's Central Station. You'll need to pay cash for your train tickets at the window, as ticket machines accept chip-and-pin cards only.

To get between Schiphol and downtown Amsterdam (10 miles away), you have several options:

Train: Direct trains to Amsterdam's Central Station run frequently from Schiphol Plaza (4-6/hour, 15 minutes, €4.30). Schiphol's train station also serves other destinations including Delft, The Hague, Rotterdam, Bruges, and Brussels.

Shuttle Bus: The Connexxion shuttle bus departs from lane A7 in front of the airport and takes you to your hotel neighborhood. There are three different routes, including one to the Westerkerk (near some of my recommended hotels). Ask the attendant which one works best for your hotel (2/hour, 20 minutes, €16 one-way, €26 round-trip). For trips from Amsterdam to Schiphol, reserve at least 2 hours ahead (tel. 088-339-4741, airporthotelshuttle.nl).

Public Bus: Bus #197 (departing from lane B9 in front of the airport) is handy for those going to the Leidseplein district (€4, buy ticket from driver). If you're staying in the city of Haarlem, catch #300 from lane B6.

Taxi: Allow about €60-70 to downtown Amsterdam.

Amsterdam's Central Train Station

Amsterdam Centraal is truly "central." You're within walking distance of Dam Square, and all the transportation options (tram, bus, taxi, metro, and rental bikes) are right out front.

The station is fully equipped for the traveler. The GWK Travelex counters act as unofficial tourist information desks and sell international phone cards. Luggage lockers are in the east corridor, under the "B" end of the platforms (€5-7/24 hours, always open). The station has two handy Albert Heijn supermarkets and plenty of eateries (especially near platform 2; try the venerable First Class Grand Café). Ticket machines accept chip-and-pin cards only; you'll need to pay cash at a ticket window.

Exiting the station, you're in the heart of the city. Straight ahead is Damrak street, leading to Dam Square (a 15-minute walk). To your left are the TI, the GVB public-transit office, and the MacBike bike rental (in the station building, ✪ see page 162). To the right of the station are the postcard-perfect neighborhoods of West Amsterdam; some of my recommended hotels are within walking distance.

The city's blue trams are easy to use—just buy a ticket or pass from conductor. Trams #1, #2, and #5 (which run to nearly all my recommended hotels) leave from in front of the station's main entrance. All trams leaving Central Station stop at Dam Square along their route. For more on the transit system, ✪ see page 163.

Arrival by Cruise Ship: The Passenger Terminal Amsterdam (PTA) is a mile east of Central Station, an easy 15-minute walk along the water. Or catch tram #26 (buy ticket from driver). A taxi to, say, the Rijksmuseum, would cost about €16.

HELPFUL HINTS

Tourist Information (TI): The Dutch name for a TI is "VVV," pronounced "fay fay fay." Amsterdam's main TIs—at Central Station and at Leidseplein—are crowded and inefficient, and the free maps are poor quality. More helpful is the call center (Mon-Fri 8:00-18:00) at tel. 020/201-8800 or 0900-400-4040 or (from the US) 011-31-20-551-2525. The TIs sell good city maps (€2.50), walking-tour brochures (€3), skip-the-line museum tickets (though it's easier buying these online), and the *Time Out Amsterdam* entertainment guide (€3). Inside Central Station, the GWK Currency Exchange offices (though not officially TIs) can answer basic tourist questions, with shorter lines (open daily until 22:00).

English Bookstores: For fiction and guidebooks, try the **American Book Center** (at Spui 12, daily 10:00-20:00, tel. 020/535-2575) or the huge and helpful **Selexyz Scheltema** (at Koningsplein 20, daily 9:30-18:00, tel. 020/523-1411).

Maps: The free map of *Amsterdam Museums: Guide to 37 Museums* is one of the best overall city maps; ask for it at big museums. The *Carto Studio Centrumkaart Amsterdam* is top-notch (€2.50). Online, check out the "Go Where the Locals Go" city map at amsterdamanything.nl.

Hurdling the Language Barrier: This is one of the easiest places in the non-English-speaking world for an English speaker. Nearly all signs and services are offered in both Dutch and English. Pronunciation, however, can be tough: Dam (pronounced dahm), Damrak (DAHM-rock), Spui (spow, rhymes with cow), Rokin (roh-KEEN), Kalverstraat (KAL-ver-straht), Leidseplein (LIDE-zuh-pline), Jordaan (yor-DAHN), and *gracht* (a canal, pronounced khrockt). To learn a few Dutch pleasantries, ✪ see page 177.

Time: The Netherlands' time zone is six/nine hours ahead of the east/west coasts of the US.

Business Hours: Most businesses are open Monday through Friday roughly 9:00-19:00, Saturday from 9:00 until mid-afternoon, and closed Sundays. The first Sunday of the month, many stores open for "shopping Sunday" *(koopzondag)*. Boutique-type shops have slightly different hours: Tuesday to Saturday 10:00-18:00, Sunday-Monday 12:00-18:00 (and some stay open until 21:00 on Thursday).

Watt's Up? Europe's electrical system is 220 volts, instead of North America's 110 volts. You'll need an adapter plug with two round prongs, sold inexpensively at travel stores in the US. Most newer electronics (such

Tipping

Tipping in the Netherlands isn't as generous as it is in the US. To tip a taxi driver, round up to the next euro (for a €4.50 fare, give €5). For longer rides, figure about 5-10 percent. At hotels, if you let the porter carry your luggage, tip a euro for each bag. For sit-down service in a restaurant, a 12-15 percent service charge is always already included in the list price of the food. However, if you feel the service was exceptional, it's fine to tip 5-10 percent extra.

as laptops, hair dryers, and battery chargers) convert automatically, so you won't need a separate converter.

Numbers and Stumblers: What Americans call the second floor of a building is the first floor in Europe. Europeans write dates as day/month/year. Commas are decimal points and vice versa—a dollar and half is 1,50, and there are 5.280 feet in a mile. The Netherlands uses the metric system: A kilogram is 2.2 pounds; a liter is about a quart; and a kilometer is six-tenths of a mile. Temperature is measured in Celsius: 0°C = 32°F. To roughly convert Celsius to Fahrenheit, double the number and add 30.

Laundry: In the Jordaan, try Clean Brothers Wasserij (Westerstraat 26, €7 self-service, €9 ready in an hour, tel. 020/627-9888). Near Leidseplein, try Powders (Kerkstraat 56, self-service or drop-off, mobile 06-2630-6057). Or ask your hotelier for the nearest location.

Pedestrian Safety: Beware of silent transportation—trams, electric mopeds, and bicycles—when walking around town. Don't walk on tram tracks or pink/maroon bicycle paths. Before you step off any sidewalk, do a double- or triple-check in both directions to make sure all's clear.

Best Views: Although sea-level Amsterdam is notoriously horizontal, there are a few high points where you can get the big picture. ✪ The best city views are from the Central Library (see page 132), the Westerkerk tower (see page 94), the Old Church (Oude Kerk, see page 74), the top floor of the Kalvertoren shopping complex (see page 29), and the rooftop terrace at the NEMO science museum (see page 133).

GETTING AROUND AMSTERDAM

I get around Amsterdam by walking, biking, and taking the occasional tram. The longest walk a tourist would make is an hour from Central Station to the Rijksmuseum. Pedestrians should be extremely vigilant for silent but potentially painful bikes, trams, and crotch-high bollards.

By Bike

Everyone—bank managers, students, pizza delivery boys, and police—uses this mode of transport. It's by far the smartest way to travel in a city that's perfectly flat, and where 40 percent of all traffic rolls on two wheels. Consider renting a bike for a few days, chain it to the rack outside your hotel at night, and enjoy wonderful mobility.

One-speed bikes, with *"brrringing"* bells, rent for about €10/day (must leave ID, deposit, or credit-card imprint). Your hotel can direct you to the nearest rental shop. Star Bikes Rental, a five-minute walk east of Central Station, is cheap (€7/day, €17/3 days, De Ruyterkade 127, tel. 020/620-3215, starbikesrental.com). MacBike, at the east end of Central Station, is the biggest (€9.50/24 hours, €19/72 hours, tel. 020/620-0985, macbike.nl).

No one here wears a helmet. They do, however, strictly obey bicycle traffic laws: Use arm signals, follow the bike-only traffic signals, stay in the obvious and omnipresent bike lanes, yield to traffic on the right, dismount and walk your bike through pedestrian zones. Fear oncoming trams. Carefully cross tram tracks at a perpendicular angle to avoid catching your tire in the rut. Bike theft is rampant—follow your rental agency's locking directions (usually involving two locks) to the letter. A handy bicycle route-planner can be found at routecraft.com (select "bikeplanner," then

click British flag for English). For a "Do-It-Yourself Bike Tour of Amsterdam" and for bike tours, see "Activities," later in this chapter.

By Tram, Bus, and Metro

Amsterdam's public transit system includes trams, buses, and an underground metro; of these, trams are most useful for most tourists. A helpful GVB public-transit information office is located in front of Central Station (Mon-Fri 7:00-21:00, Sat-Sun 10:00-18:00, gvb.nl).

Tickets: A single ticket costs €2.80 and is good for one hour on the tram, bus, and metro, including transfers. You can board any tram or bus and buy a ticket from the conductor with no extra fee. Given how expensive single tickets are, consider getting a pass: A 24-hour pass is €7.50 (€12/48 hours, €16.50/72 hours, €21/96 hours). Tickets and passes are sold on board, at metro-station vending machines (cash or European credit card only), at GVB public-transit offices, and at TIs. Note that the I amsterdam sightseeing card (page 168) includes a transit pass. If you're staying for a week or more, look into the OV-Chipkaart, a prepaid card covering all of the Netherlands' buses and trams (non-refundable €7.50 deposit, ov-chipkaart.nl).

Riding the Trams: Board at any door not marked with a red/white "do not enter" sticker. If you need a ticket or pass, pay the conductor (in a booth at the back); if there's no conductor, pay the driver in front. You must always "check in" as you board by scanning your ticket or pass at the pink-and-gray scanner, and "check out" by scanning it again when you get off. The scanner will beep and flash a green light after a successful scan. Don't accidentally scan twice while boarding, or it becomes invalid. To exit, press a green button to open the doors.

Trams #2 (*Nieuw Sloten*) and #5 (*A'veen Binnenhof*) travel the north-south axis, from Central Station to Dam Square to Leidseplein to Museumplein (Van Gogh and Rijks museums). Tram #1 (marked *Osdorp*) also runs to Leidseplein. At Central Station, these three trams depart from the west side of Stationsplein (with the station behind you, they're to your right).

Tram #14, which doesn't connect to Central Station, goes east-west (Westerkerk-Dam Square-Muntplein-Waterlooplein-Plantage). If you get lost in Amsterdam, don't sweat it—10 of the city's 17 trams take you back to Central Station.

Buses and Metro: Though few tourists use the bus and metro, they work the same as on the trams—scan your ticket or pass as you enter and again when you leave. The metro system is scant—used mostly for commuting to the suburbs—but it does connect Central Station with some sights east of Damrak (Nieuwmarkt-Waterlooplein-Weesperplein).

Other Transport

Taxi: Amsterdam is not a good town for taxis, thanks to circuitous streets and pricey fares. The drop charge is a steep €7.50 for the first two kilometers (e.g., from Central Station to the Mint Tower), after which it's €2.30 per kilometer. On the other hand, there's no extra fee for luggage, and you can sometimes bargain down to a lower rate. Wave taxis down, find a rare taxi stand, or call 020/677-7777.

Bike Taxis: These hard-working entrepreneurs (found particularly near Dam Square and Leidseplein) wheel you wherever you want. But negotiate the price before you board (no meter). Typical fares are €1/3 minutes, no surcharge for baggage (Leidseplein to Anne Frank House is about €6).

Tourist Canal Boats: Though most canal boats are meant for round-trip sightseeing cruises, a few companies make stops along the way that can work well for point-to-point travel. Check the brochures or websites for Canal Hopper (tel. 020/626-5574, canal.nl), Rederij Lovers (tel. 020/530-1090, lovers.nl), or Canal Bus (tel. 020/623-9886, canal.nl). For basic tourist sightseeing rides, see "Activities," later in this chapter.

By Car: If you've got a car, park it—all you'll find are frustrating one-way streets, terrible parking, and meter maids with a passion for booting cars. Park in a central garage (€60/day), or at a park-and-ride lot on the outskirts (follow *P&R* signs from freeway, €8/24 hours) and take transit into the city center. Ask your hotel for parking advice.

COMMUNICATING

Telephones

Making Calls: To call the Netherlands from the US or Canada: Dial 011 (our international access code) + 31 (the Netherlands' country code) + the local number, without the initial zero. To call the Netherlands from a European country: Dial 00 (Europe's international access code) + 31 followed by the local number, without the initial zero. To call within the Netherlands: If you're dialing within an area code, you don't need to include the three-digit code (that always starts with a 0). If you're dialing from outside the area code, you must include the three-digit code (including the initial zero). To call from the Netherlands to another country: Dial 00, the country code (for example, 1 for the US or Canada), then the area code and number. If you're calling European countries whose phone numbers begin with 0, you'll usually have to omit that 0 when you dial. If you're calling from Europe using your US mobile phone, you may need to dial as if you're calling from the US.

Phoning Inexpensively: Since coin-op pay phones are virtually obsolete, you'll need an international phone card (€5). With this, you can make reasonably priced local and international calls from any pay phone, from a European mobile phone, and even from your hotel phone (though some hotels block these cards or charge a fee). Buy cards at newsstands, electronics stores, and Internet cafés. Tell the vendor where you'll be

---

Useful Phone Numbers

Police: Tel. 112
Emergency Medical Assistance: Tel. 112
US Consulate: In Amsterdam, tel. 020/575-5309, after-hours emergency tel. 070/310-2209, Museumplein 19, must make appointment at amsterdam.usconsulate.gov
US Embassy: In The Hague, tel. 070/310-2209, visits by appointment only, Lange Voorhout 102, netherlands.usembassy.gov
Canadian Embassy: In The Hague, tel. 070/311-1600, consular services Mon-Fri 9:30-13:00, closed Sat-Sun, Sophialaan 7, canada.nl
Collect Calls to the US: Tel. 0800-022-9111

making the most calls (to America), and he'll select a good-value brand. When using an international phone card, you always must dial the area code, even if you're calling across the street. Calling from your hotel room without a phone card can be a rip-off—ask your hotelier about their rates before you dial.

Mobile Phones and Smartphones: Many US mobile phones work in Europe. Expect to pay around $1.50 a minute for phone calls and 30 cents per text message (somewhat less if you sign up for an international calling plan with your service provider). It's easy to buy a phone in Europe, which costs more up front but is cheaper by the call. You'll find mobile-phone stores selling cheap phones (for as little as $20 plus minutes) and SIM cards, at Schiphol Airport, Central Station, and throughout Amsterdam.

Smartphones give you access to the Internet and travel-oriented apps—helpful for planning your sightseeing, emailing hotels, and staying in touch. You can make free or cheap phone calls using Skype (sign up at skype.com), Google Talk (google.com/talk), or Facetime (preloaded on many Apple devices).

To avoid sky-high fees for data roaming, disable data roaming entirely, and only go online when you have Wi-Fi (e.g., at your hotel or in a café). Or you could sign up for an international data plan for the duration of your trip: $30 typically buys about 100 megabytes—enough to view 100 websites or send/receive 1,000 emails.

For more information, talk to your service provider or see ricksteves. com/phoning.

Internet Access and Wi-Fi

Most hotels offer some form of free or cheap Internet access—either a shared computer in the lobby or Wi-Fi in the room. Otherwise, your hotelier can point you to the nearest Internet café. You'll also find Wi-Fi hotspots at many cafés (namely, establishments that sell coffee, bagels, etc). Places called "coffeeshops," which sell marijuana, also commonly offer Internet access—letting you surf with a special bravado.

The best place for serious surfing is the towering Central Library (the Openbare Bibliotheek Amsterdam), which has hundreds of fast terminals and Wi-Fi (€1/30 minutes, daily 10:00-22:00, a 10-minute walk east of the train station). The café across the street from Central Station (next to the TI) also has pay Internet access and Wi-Fi.

SIGHTSEEING TIPS

Hours: Hours of sights can change unexpectedly, so confirm the latest times from a TI, or at the sight's website, or the general website **iamsterdam.com.** Many sights stop admitting people 30-60 minutes before closing time, and guards start shooing people out before the actual closing time, so don't save the best for last.

What to Expect: Important sights such as the Rijksmuseum have metal detectors or conduct bag searches that will slow your entry. Many of Amsterdam's sights require you to check even small daypacks and coats—usually for free, often in coin-op lockers where you get your coin back.

Photos and videos are normally allowed, but flashes or tripods usually are not. Many sights offer guided tours and rent audioguides (€4-7). Expect changes—artwork can be in restoration or on tour. Most have an on-site café.

Discounts: Many sights offer free or reduced admission for children under 18 and for students (with International Student Identity Cards, isic. org). Senior discounts are generally only for EU residents, but it's worth asking.

Free Rick Steves Audio Tours: I've produced free audio tours of many of Amsterdam's best sights. With a mobile device, you can take me along for the Amsterdam City Walk, the Jordaan Walk, or the Red Light District Walk. Download them via the Rick Steves Audio Europe smartphone app, ricksteves.com/audioeurope, iTunes, or Google Play.

Advance Tickets and Sightseeing Cards

You can avoid long ticket lines (common from late March-Oct) at the Rijksmuseum, Van Gogh Museum, and Anne Frank House by booking tickets in advance or getting a sightseeing pass. (But note that nobody can skip security lines.) If you're visiting off-season, it's less important to worry about line-skipping options, especially if you use my other crowd-beating tips.

Advance Tickets: It's easy to buy tickets online through each museum's website, generally with no extra booking fee. You just print out your ticket and bring it to the ticket-holder's line for a quick entry. You can also buy advance tickets at TIs (though lines there can be long). Another line-skipping option is a sightseeing pass. Read on...

Museumkaart (€50): This sightseeing pass—which covers many museums throughout the Netherlands for a year—can save money and time for heavy-duty sightseers. For example, if you visit the Rijksmuseum, Van Gogh Museum, Anne Frank House, and Amsterdam Museum, the pass would almost pay for itself right there. Plus, it lets you skip the ticket lines (except at the Anne Frank House). Check amsterdam.info for a list of which sights are included, and do the math. The Museumkaart is sold at all participating museums—buy it at a less-crowded one to avoid lines.

Other Sightseeing Passes: Though not as good a deal for most people, the **I amsterdam Card** covers many Amsterdam sights (including a canal boat ride) and includes a transportation pass. But it does not cover the Rijksmuseum, the Anne Frank House, or any museums outside Amsterdam, and it lets you skip lines only at the Van Gogh Museum. Get details at iamsterdamcard.com. Another pass you'll see advertised, the Holland Pass, is not worth it.

THEFT AND EMERGENCIES

Theft: While violent crime is rare in the city center, thieves (mainly pickpockets) thrive near famous monuments, on public transportation, at places of drunkenness, in hostels, or anywhere crowds press together. Be alert to the possibility of theft, even when you're absorbed in the wonder and newness of Amsterdam. Smartphones are thief-magnets. So are rental bikes (✪ see page 162). I keep my valuables—passport, credit cards, crucial documents, and large amounts of cash—in a money belt that I tuck under my beltline. Dial 112 for English-speaking police help. To replace a passport, file the police report, then call your consulate or embassy to make an appointment (US consulate, tel. 020/575-5309, amsterdam.us-consulate.gov).

Medical Help: Dial 112 for a medical emergency. Most doctors speak English. For minor ailments, do as the Dutch do and first visit a pharmacy, where qualified technicians routinely diagnose and prescribe. There's a one-stop-shopping pharmacy near Leidseplein named "DA" Dienstdoende Apotheek (Leidsestraat 74-76, daily until 22:00, tel. 020/627-5351) and another near Dam Square, called BENU Apotheek (Damstraat 2, daily until 17:00, tel. 020/624-4331). Otherwise, ask your hotelier for assistance.

ACTIVITIES

Shopping

Amsterdam brings out the browser, even in those who were not born to shop. Modish boutiques, open-air markets, quirky souvenirs, and pleasant neighborhoods can make window-shopping a ▲▲▲ sightseeing experience.

Most shops are open Tuesday-Saturday 10:00-18:00, Sunday-Monday 12:00-18:00, and some stay open until 21:00 on Thursdays. The TIs have a free *Shopping in Amsterdam* brochure.

Department Stores: For essential items, try two all-purpose chain stores open until 19:00 or later—Hema (at Central Station and Kalverstraat 212) or Vroom & Dreesmann (Kalverstraat 203). The De Bijenkorf department store on Dam Square is old-time fancy, with a little view café on the first floor. The Magna Plaza (a block west of Dam Square) is a stylish mall of 40 boutiques.

Shopping Neighborhoods: The central axis of streets from Central Station to Leidseplein—essentially, the route of the Amsterdam City Walk—is the busiest shopping corridor in town. It includes Kalverstraat (pedestrian-only but soulless) and Leidsestraat (with trendy, elegant shops).

In West Amsterdam, the **Jordaan,** with its main drag Westerstraat, is a veritable wonderland of funky, artsy shops (especially on Monday, when a street market appears nearby). **The Nine Little Streets** (De Negen Straatjes) is a tic-tac-toe of streets that's home to 190 diverse shops and trendy cafés. The center is approximately where Wolvenstraat crosses the Keizersgracht and Herengracht canals (just west of the Amsterdam Museum). **Prinsheerlijk**—located a looooong block north of the Anne Frank House on Prinsenstraat—has high-end shops.

The Southwest Amsterdam (Museumplein) neighborhood has two of the city's ritziest zones. **Spiegelkwartier** (stretching north from the Rijksmuseum along Spiegelgracht and Nieuwe Spiegelstraat) is *the* place for art and antiques. **P. C. Hooftstraat** is the city's most expensive shopping street, located between Museumplein and Vondelpark.

Open-Air Markets: These are museums for people-watchers. Ten general markets, open six days a week (generally 9:30-17:00, closed Sun), keep folks who brake for garage sales pulling U-turns. Try the flower market near the Mint Tower (✪ see page 29). The Waterlooplein Flea Market (daily except Sun near Waterlooplein metro station) has stalls of garage-sale junk/treasure. The huge Albert Cuyp street market is Amsterdam's biggest, bustling Monday to Saturday 9:00-17:00. You'll find fish, exotic vegetables, bolts of fabric, pantyhose, bargain clothes, native Dutch and ethnic food stands (especially *stroopwafels* and Surinamese *rotis*), and great people-watching. It's located a 10-minute walk east of Museumplein and a block south of the Heineken Experience (tram #16 or #24).

Souvenirs: You won't need a guidebook to find plenty of shops selling wooden shoes, blue-and-white delftware (ranging from inexpensive fireplace titles to very expensive antiques), *jenever* (Dutch gin made from juniper berries, sold in traditional stone bottles), chocolate (Verkade or Droste cocoa in tins), or flower seeds and bulbs (be sure they're US Customs-friendly).

Art-themed items (Rembrandt posters, Van Gogh coffee mugs) are popular—try the Van Gogh Museum bookshop. Amsterdam's rare bookstores have old books and maps. Marijuana pipes must be absolutely clean and unused to get through US Customs (and even then they may hassle you on legal technicalities). To mail your purchases home, ask your hotelier for the nearest ersatz post office, or use Service Point, a shipping service at Schiphol Airport.

Getting a VAT Refund: If you purchase more than €175 worth of goods at a single store, you may be eligible to get a refund of the 20 percent Value-Added Tax (VAT). Have the store fill out the paperwork, then get it stamped at the airport by Customs and processed by a VAT refund company (e.g., Global Blue or Premier Tax/Travelex, located in Schiphol's departure halls). Get more details from your merchant or see ricksteves.com/vat.

Customs for American Shoppers: You are allowed to take home $800 worth of items per person duty-free, once every 30 days. You can also bring in duty-free a liter of alcohol. As for food, you can take home many processed and packaged foods (e.g., vacuum-packed cheeses, chocolate, mustard) but no fresh produce or meats. Any liquid-containing foods must be packed in checked luggage, a potential recipe for disaster. To check customs rules and duty rates, visit help.cbp.gov.

Nightlife

Many Amsterdam hotels serve breakfast until 11:00 because so many people—visitors and locals—live for nighttime in this city.

On summer evenings, people flock to the main squares for drinks at outdoor tables. **Leidseplein** is the liveliest square, surrounded by theaters, restaurants, and nightclubs. The slightly quieter **Rembrandtplein** (with adjoining Thorbeckeplein and nearby Reguliersdwarsstraat) is the center of gay clubs and nightlife. **Spui** features a full city block of bars. The **Red Light District** (particularly Oudezijds Achterburgwal) is less sleazy, even festive, in the early evening (before 22:00).

For a list of current events, try *Time Out Amsterdam* (a magazine sold at newsstands, or timeout.com). The free, irreverent *Boom!* brochure also has many handy tips for newbies (available at TIs and many bars). *Uitkrant* magazine is in Dutch, but anyone can figure out an event and its date, time, and location (available at TIs, bars, and bookstores).

The AUB/Last Minute Ticket Shop at Stadsschouwburg Theater is the best one-stop-shopping box office for theater, classical music, and major rock shows. The Last Minute window sells half-price, same-day tickets to certain shows; half-price sales start at noon (Mon-Fri 10:00-19:00, Sat 10:00-18:00, Sun 12:00-18:00, Leidseplein 26, tel. 0900-0191—€0.40/minute, lastminuteticketshop.nl).

Classical Music: The Concertgebouw is the main venue, located

at the far south end of Museumplein (free 12:30 lunch concerts on Wed, tel. 0900-671-8345, concertgebouw.nl). For chamber music and contemporary works, visit the Muziekgebouw aan 't IJ, near the train station (Piet Heinkade 1, tel. 020/788-2000, muziekgebouw.nl). For opera and dance, try the "Stopera" at Waterlooplein 22 (tel. 020/625-5455). In the summer, Vondelpark hosts open-air concerts.

The Westerkerk has free lunchtime concerts on Fridays at 13:00 (April-Oct only, Prinsengracht 281, tel. 020/624-7766, westerkerk.nl). The New Church on Dam Square occasionally offers organ concerts (tel. 020/638-6909, nieuwekerk.nl). The Red Light District's Old Church (Oude Kerk) has carillon concerts Tuesday at 14:00 and Saturday at 16:00 (Oudekerksplein, tel. 020/625-8284, oudekerk.nl).

Rock, Jazz, Hip-Hop: Two clubs near Leidseplein present bigname acts that you might recognize...if you're younger than I am: Melkweg (Lijnbaansgracht 234a, tel. 020/531-8181, melkweg.nl) and Paradiso (Weteringschans 6, tel. 020/626-4521, paradiso.nl). Jazz has a long tradition at the Bimhuis nightclub, now located at the Muziekgebouw by Central

Station (Piet Heinkade 3, great views from the bar, tel. 020/788-2188, bimhuis.nl).

Boom Chicago: This R-rated comedy improv act (in English) has been entertaining tourists and locals for years, with raucous skits about Dutch culture and local tourism. It erupts nightly at the theater at Rozengracht 117 (€22-26, ticket office open Wed-Sat from 13:00, no Mon shows Jan-March, tel. 020/423-0101, boomchicago.nl).

Theater: Amsterdam is one of the world centers for experimental live theater (much of it in English). Many theaters cluster around the street called the Nes, which stretches south from Dam Square.

Movies: Many theaters run movies in their original language. It's not unusual for showings to be sold out—consider buying tickets during the day. Two memorable places to see a movie are the classic Tuschinski Theater (✪ see page 126) and the splashy EYE Film Institute (✪ page 134).

Late-Night Museums: The Anne Frank House is always open until at least 19:00, and until 22:00 on some occasions. The Stedelijk Museum stays open until 22:00 on Thursday, and the Van Gogh Museum is open until 22:00 on Friday. Amsterdam's marijuana and sex museums are always open until at least 23:00.

Marijuana (a.k.a. Cannabis)

Smoking marijuana—for all intents and purposes—is legal in Amsterdam. You can buy it in licensed "coffeeshops" and smoke it there. By law, the prospective customer has to initiate the transaction by asking the bartender to show them the cannabis menu or display case. Shops generally sell pre-rolled joints (€3-5) and baggies (€10-15). There are different strains ("Mellow Yellow," "Thai Guy"), and you can buy either hashish (the dried sap of the cannabis plant) or the leaf of the plant (which the Dutch call "marihuana" or "grass").

Most shops have loaner bongs or rolling papers. You can smoke your marijuana in any coffeeshop (regardless of where you bought it), so long as you buy a drink or snack. There are always new proposals afloat to try to ban marijuana—stay tuned.

Of Amsterdam's many coffeeshops, here are a few that have a mellow atmosphere that's welcoming to first-time Americans: Paradox is the most *gezellig* (cozy), a graceful place that also serves light meals (two blocks west of Anne Frank House at Eerste Bloemdwarsstraat 2, tel. 020/623-5639, paradoxcoffeeshop.com). The Grey Area is two blocks east of the

Practicalities

Anne Frank House (Oude Leliestraat 2, tel. 020/420-4301, greyarea.nl). The Bulldog Café is the big franchise brand, with one right on Leidseplein (Leidseplein 17, tel. 020/625-6278, thebulldog.com).

Canal Boat Tours

These long, low, tourist-laden boats offer a relaxing one-hour introduction to the city (with uninspiring recorded headphone commentary). Several different companies offer similar services: Boats depart every 15-30 minutes from various docks around town. Some operate only by day (generally 10:00-18:00), but some have night cruises, when bridges are illuminated. Choose your boat company based on convenience of its starting point. Tip: Boats leave only when full, so jump on a full boat to avoid waiting at the dock.

Rederij P. Kooij is cheapest, located at the corner of Spui and Rokin streets, about 10 minutes from Dam Square (€9, boats until 22:00 in summer, tel. 020/623-3810, rederijkooij.nl). Blue Boat Company is near Leidseplein (€14, last regular cruise at 19:00 in summer, €17.50 night cruises until 22:00 by reservation, Stadhouderskade 30, tel. 020/679-1370, blueboat.nl). Holland International is opposite Central Station (€14, nightly until 22:00; Prins Hendrikkade 33a, tel. 020/625-3035, hir.nl).

The smaller Canal Hopper boats offer live guides and make stops, allowing you to hop on and hop off for sightseeing at, e.g., the Anne Frank House, Rijksmuseum, or Red Light District (€24 day pass, €17 round-trip ticket, daily 10:00-17:00, only Fri-Sun Sept-June, tel. 020/626-5574, canal.nl).

Paddleboats: For do-it-yourself canal tours and lots of exercise, rent these "canal bikes" from Canal Bus, near the Anne Frank House, Rijksmuseum, and Leidseplein (€8/hour per person, daily July-Aug 10:00-22:00, Sept-June 10:00-18:00).

Do-It-Yourself Bike Tour of Amsterdam

For a good day trip enjoying the bridges, bike lanes, and sleepy, off-the-beaten-path canals, try this route:

Start at Central Station. Head west down Haarlemmerstraat, working your wide-eyed way down Prinsengracht (drop into Café 't Papeneiland at Prinsengracht 2) and de-touring through the small, gentrified streets of the Jordaan neighborhood before popping out at the Westerkerk under the tallest spire in the city.

Pedal south to the lush and peaceful Vondelpark, then cut back through the center of town: Leidseplein, the Mint Tower, and along Rokin street to Dam Square. From there, cruise the Red Light District, following Oudezijds Voorburgwal past the Old Church (Oude Kerk) to Zeedijk street, and return to the train station.

To extend your ride, you catch a free ferry (free for both you and your bike) to the north bank of the North Sea Canal. Behind Central Station are docks with four ferries, leaving every few minutes. The middle two ferries shuttle immediately across the harbor (a 3-minute ride). From there, you can ride your bike two kilometers (1.25 miles) along the canal, through suburbs, and into the *polderland* and villages. Amsterdam is gone, and you're rolling through your very own Dutch painting.

Guided Tours

For a two-hour group tour that gives a once-over of central Amsterdam, try the knowledgeable Adam's Apple Tours (€25, leaves from Central Station, tel. 020/616-7867) or the enthusiastic-but-amateur New Europe "Free" Tours (truly free but tips expected, leave from Dam Square, new europetours.eu).

If you'd like a private guide to anywhere in Amsterdam, Albert Walet is

likeable and knowledgeable (€70/2 hours for up to 4 people, mobile 06-2069-7882, abwalet@yahoo.com). In the Red Light District, Randy Roy's Red Light Tours offers group tours nightly at 20:00 that are fun and informative (€15, mobile 06-4185-3288, randyroysredlighttours.com).

Guided Bike Tours: Yellow Bike Guided Tours takes groups of people on a variety of two- to three-hour routes, either in-city or to the countryside (€20-30, bike rental included, leave from Nieuwezijds Kolk 29 near Central Station (reservations smart, tel. 020/620-6940, yellowbike.nl). Joy Ride Bike Tours offers private 4-hour tours as well as custom theme tours, starting near the Rijksmuseum (€26-30, mobile 06-4361-1798, joyridetours.nl).

r'cksteves.com

This Pocket guide is one of dozens of titles in my series of guidebooks on European travel. I also produce a public television series, *Rick Steves' Europe*, and a public radio show, *Travel with Rick Steves*. My website, ricksteves.com, offers a wealth of free travel information including videos and podcasts of my shows, audio tours of Europe's great sights, travel forums, guidebook updates, my travel blog, and my guide to European rail passes—plus an online travel store and information on our tours of Europe.

How Was Your Trip? If you'd like to share your tips, concerns, and discoveries after using this book, please fill out the survey at ricksteves.com/feedback. It helps us and fellow travelers.

Dutch Phrases

You won't need to learn Dutch, but at least learn a few pleasantries to connect with the locals.

The all-purpose word *alstublieft* (AHL-stoo-bleeft) can mean "please," "thanks," or "You're welcome."

English	Dutch	Pronunciation
Hello.	Hallo.	hol-LOH
Good day.	Dag.	dahh
Good morning.	Goeiemorgen.	hhhoy-ah MOR-hhhen
Yes	Ja	yah
No	Nee	nay
Please	Alstublieft	AHL-stoo-bleeft
Thank you.	Dank u wel.	dahnk yoo vehl
Excuse me.	Pardon.	par-DOHN
Do you speak English?	Spreekt u Engels?	spraykt oo ENG-els
Goodbye.	Tot ziens.	toht zeens
one / two / three	een / twee / drie	ayn / t'vay / dree
What does it cost?	Wat kost?	vaht kost
I would like...	Ik wil graag...	ik vil hhhrahhhk
...a room.	...een kamer.	un kah-mer
...a ticket.	...een kaart.	un kart
...a bike.	...een fiets.	un feets
Where is...?	Waar is...?	vahr is
...the station	...het station	het sta-tsee-on
...the tourist info office	...de VVV	duh fay fay fay
left / right	links / rechts	links / rechts
open / closed	open / gesloten	"open" / hhhe-sloh-ten
menu	menu	muh-NOO
with / without	met / buiten	met / bow-ten
and / or	en / of	en / of
bread	brood	broht
salad	sla	slah
cheese	kaas	kahs
water	water	WAH-tuhr
beer	bier	beer
wine	wijn	wayn
coffee	koffie	"coffee"
tea	thee	tay
I am vegetarian.	Ik ben vegetarish.	ik ben vay-hhhe-tah-rish
Tasty.	Lekker.	lek-ker
Enjoy!	Smakelijk!	smak-kuh-luk
Cheers!	Proost!	prohst
The bill, please.	De rekening, alstublieft.	duh RAY-kun-ing AHL-stoo-bleeft

INDEX

Index

PHOTO CREDITS

Join a Rick Steves tour

Enjoy Europe's warmest welcome... with the flexibility and friendship of a small group getting to know Rick's favorite places and people. It all starts with our free tour catalog and DVD.

Great guides, small groups, no grumps.

Start your trip at

Free information and great gear to

▶ Plan Your Trip

Browse thousands of articles and a wealth of money-saving tips for planning your dream trip. You'll find up-to-date information on Europe's best destinations, packing smart, getting around, finding rooms, staying healthy, avoiding scams and more.

▶ Eurail Passes

Find out, step-by-step, if a railpass makes sense for your trip—and how to avoid buying more than you need. Get a bunch of free extras!

▶ Graffiti Wall & Travelers Helpline

Learn, ask, share—our online community of savvy travelers is a great resource for first-time travelers to Europe, as well as seasoned pros.

Rick Steves' Europe Through the Back Door, Inc.

Rick Steves. www.ricksteves.com

Avalon Travel
a member of the Perseus Books Group
1700 Fourth Street
Berkeley, CA 94710

Printed in China by RR Donnelley
First printing July 2014

ISBN 978-1-59880-384-6
ISSN 2333-5491

For the latest on Rick's lectures, guidebooks, tours, public radio show, and public television series, contact Europe Through the Back Door, 130 Fourth Avenue North, Edmonds, WA 98020, tel. 425/771-8303, fax 425/771-0833, ricksteves.com, or rick@ricksteves.com.

Rick Steves' Europe Through the Back Door
Managing Editor: Risa Laib
Editorial & Production Manager: Jennifer Madison Davis
Editors: Glenn Eriksen, Tom Griffin, Cameron Hewitt, Suzanne Kotz, Cathy Lu, Carrie Shepherd
Researcher: Tom Griffin
Maps & Graphics: Barb Geisler, Sandra Hundacker, David C. Hoerlein, Lauren Mills, Mary Rostad

Avalon Travel
Senior Editor and Series Manager: Madhu Prasher
Editor: Jamie Andrade
Assistant Editor: Maggie Ryan
Copy Editor: Denise Silva
Proofreader: Rebecca Freed
Indexer: Stephen Callahan
Production & Typesetting: McGuire Barber Design
Cover Design: Kimberly Glyder Design
Interior Design: Darren Alessi
Maps & Graphics: Kat Bennett, Lohnes + Wright
Photography: Rick Steves, Steve Smith, David C. Hoerlein, Gene Openshaw, Laura VanDeventer, Cameron Hewitt, Julie Coen, Barb Geisler, Ben Cameron, Ragen Van Sewell, Robyn Cronin, Rob Unck, Carol Ries, Rich Earl, Rachel Worthman (additional photo credits, page 187)
Front Cover Image: left, statue of Rembrandt van Rijn © Richard Wareham Fotografie/Getty Images; right, Keizersgracht © Fraser Hall/Getty Images

ABOUT THE AUTHORS

Rick Steves

Since 1973, Rick Steves has spent 100 days every year exploring Europe. Along with writing and researching a bestselling series of guidebooks, Rick produces a public television series *(Rick Steves' Europe)*, a public radio show *(Travel with Rick Steves)*, and an app and podcast *(Rick Steves Audio Europe);* writes a nationally syndicated newspaper column; organizes guided tours that take over ten thousand travelers to Europe annually; and offers an information-packed website (www.ricksteves.com). With the help of his hard-working staff of 80 at Europe Through the Back Door—in Edmonds, Washington, just north of Seattle—Rick's mission is to make European travel fun, affordable, and culturally enlightening for Americans.

Connect with Rick: ☷ facebook.com/RickSteves twitter: @RickSteves

Gene Openshaw

Gene Openshaw is a writer, composer, tour guide, and lecturer on art and history. Specializing in writing walking tours of Europe's cultural sights, Gene has co-authored a dozen of Rick's books and contributes to Rick's public television series. As a composer, Gene has written a full-length opera *(Matter),* a violin sonata, and dozens of songs. He lives near Seattle with his daughter, and roots for the Mariners in good times and bad.

FOLDOUT COLOR MAP

The foldout map on the opposite page includes:
• A map of Amsterdam on one side
• Maps of Greater Amsterdam and the Netherlands on the other side